Christmas
Slow Cooking

Christmas
Slow Cooking

Over 250 Hassle-Free Holiday Recipes for the Electric Slow Cooker

Dominique DeVito

CIDER MILL
PRESS

BOOK
PUBLISHERS

Kennebunkport, Maine

13-Digit ISBN: 978-1604333589
10-Digit ISBN: 16044333588

This book may be ordered by mail from the publisher. Please include $3.95 for postage and handling.
Please support your local bookseller first!

Books published by Cider Mill Press Book Publishers are available at special discounts for bulk purchases in the United States by corporations, institutions, and other organizations. For more information, please contact the publisher.

Cider Mill Press Book Publishers
"Where good books are ready for press"
12 Port Farm Road
Kennebunkport, Maine 04046

Visit us on the Web!
www.cidermillpress.com

Design by Alicia Freile, Tango Media
Typeset by Gwen Galeone, Tango Media
Typography: Archer, Chaparral Pro, Helvetica Neue and Voluta
All images used under license from Shutterstock.com.
Printed in China

1 2 3 4 5 6 7 8 9 0
First Edition

Contents

Introduction

Make All Your Christmas Favorites—Easier!

*I*t's that magical time of year again. As October turns to November and then to December, the days and weeks fill up with special gatherings. From school parties to work potlucks to family gatherings, to the most special gatherings—Christmas Eve, Christmas morning, and Christmas day—there's one common element. Food! Everyone wants to taste the flavors of the holidays.

Between the extra-special dinners, the festive invites, and the everyday meals, menu planning can get tricky. In months filled with shopping, decorating, wrapping presents, and entertaining, who has time to slave over the stove?

No one.

But thanks to your slow cooker and these recipes, holiday cooking—and eating—can be simple.

You won't have to baste, or share oven or stovetop space with other dishes, or worry about burning anything, or be stuck at home the whole time dinner is cooking. If you've only prepared meats, soups, or stews in the slow cooker, you are in for multiple treats as you learn to prepare breakfasts, desserts, and a variety of side dishes. You'll find recipes for

everything from Christmas favorites like baked ham, prime rib, mashed potatoes, and fruitcake to extravagances like chocolate mousse and duck confit, to yummy classics like sausage-and-egg breakfast casserole, or artichoke and spinach dip, short ribs, chicken stew, and mushroom risotto.

Learn to make risotto without having to be the only one in the kitchen, stirring constantly, while the rest of the party gathers round the fire in the other room. Wake up Christmas morning to overnight eggnog-cranberry steel-cut oatmeal. Indulge in a citrus-cinnamon spiced ham for dinner. And proudly pass apricot glazed chicken wings at your company potluck.

We've got a recipe for baked ziti that doesn't even require that you cook the pasta before putting it in the slow cooker. Some sauce, the pasta, some cheese, and you come home 6 to 8 hours later to a marvelous baked ziti. And it is delicious enough to take to a party, too.

The slow cooker is also a great tool for making the best holiday drinks—for everything from mulled wine to steamy white Russians. Any and all of these make for great fireside fare, or a way to keep a large batch of something special warmed up for carolers, the guys who put up your lights, or the neighbors who help you shovel after a snowstorm.

With this book, you'll learn to really use the slow cooker. You'll get a feel for cooking times, amount of liquids, and what to throw in when. You'll grow more comfortable experimenting with ingredients, including spices. You'll discover that, just like wrapping presents or making lists or heading out with your family to look at the light displays in the neighborhood, you'll be counting on your slow cooker to help create the kinds of memories that these moments are all about.

You might even ask Santa for another slow cooker.

Chapter 1

Slow Going:

A Guide to Slow Cookers and the Wonders of Slow Cooking

*L*uckily for all of us who are "science challenged," it doesn't take a degree in physics to operate a slow cooker. It's about the easiest machine there is on the market. It's certainly far less complicated than an espresso machine or even a waffle maker. In this chapter you'll learn about slow cookers and how to get the best results from them.

Slow cookers are inexpensive to operate; they use about as much electricity as a 60-watt bulb. They are also as easy to operate as flipping on a light switch.

Slow cookers operate by cooking food using indirect heat at a low temperature for an extended period of time. Here's the difference: Direct heat is the power of a stove burner underneath a pot, while indirect heat is the overall heat that surrounds foods as they bake in the oven.

You can purchase a slow cooker for as little as $20 at a discount store, while the top-of-the-line ones sell for more than $200. They all function in the same simple way; what increases the cost is the "bells and whistles" factors. Slow cookers come in both round and oval shapes, but they operate the same regardless of shape.

Food is assembled in a pottery insert that fits inside a metal housing and is topped with a clear lid. The food cooks from the heat generated by the circular heating wires encased between the slow cooker's outer and inner layers of metal. The coils never directly touch the crockery insert. As the element heats, it gently warms the air between the two layers of metal, and it is the hot air that touches the pottery. This construction method eliminates the need for stirring because no part of the pot gets hotter than any other.

On the front of this metal casing is the control knob. All slow cookers have Low and High settings, and most also have a Stay Warm position. Some new machines have a programmable option that enables you to start food on High and then the slow cooker automatically reduces the heat to Low after a programmed time.

The largest variation in slow cookers is their size, which range from tiny 1-quart models that are excellent for hot dips and fondue but fairly useless for anything else to gigantic 7-quart models that are excellent for large families and large batches.

Most of the recipes in this book were written for and tested in a 4- or 5-quart slow cooker; that is what is meant by *medium*. Either of those sizes makes enough for four to eight people, depending on the recipe. In a few cases, such as for lamb shanks that take up a lot of room as they cook, a large slow cooker is specified.

Rival introduced the first slow cooker, the Crock-Pot, in 1971, and the introductory slogan remains true more than 35 years later: It "cooks all day while the cook's away." Like such trademarked names as Kleenex for paper tissue or Formica for plastic laminate, Crock-Pot has almost become synonymous with the slow cooker. However, not all slow cookers are Crock-Pots, so the generic term is used in this book.

Slow Cookers and Food Safety

Questions always arise as to the safety of slow cookers. The Food Safety and Inspection Service of the U.S. Department of Agriculture approves slow cooking as a method for safe food preparation. The lengthy cooking and the steam created within the tightly covered pot combine to destroy any bacteria that might be present in the food. But you do have to be careful.

It's far more common for food-borne illness to start with meat, poultry, and seafood than from contaminated fruits and vegetables. That is why it's not wise to cook whole chickens or cuts of meat larger than those specified in the recipes in this book because during slow cooking, these large items remain too long in the bacterial "danger zone"— between 40°F and 140°F. It is important that food reaches the higher temperature in less than two hours and remains at more than 140°F for at least 30 minutes.

If you want to cook large roasts, brown them under the oven broiler or in a skillet on top of the stove over direct heat before you place them into the slow cooker. This will help the chilled meat heat up faster as well as produce a dish that is more visually appealing. Also begin with liquid that is boiling.

Getting a jump-start on dinner while you're preparing breakfast may seem like a Herculean task, and it is possible to prep the ingredients destined for the slow cooker the night before—with some limitations. If you cut meat or vegetables in advance, store them separately in the refrigerator and layer them in the slow cooker in the morning. However, do not store the cooker insert in the refrigerator because that will also increase the amount of time it takes to heat the food to a temperature that kills bacteria.

Concern about food safety extends to after a meal is cooked and the leftovers are ready for storage. As long as the temperature remains 140°F or higher, food will stay safe for many hours in the slow cooker. Leftovers, however, should never be refrigerated in the crockery insert because it will take them too long to go through the "danger zone" in the other direction—from hot to cold.

Freeze or refrigerate leftovers in shallow containers within two hours after a dish has finished cooking. Also, food should never be reheated in the slow cooker because it takes too long for chilled food to reheat. Bacteria are a problem on cooked food as well as raw ingredients. The slow cooker can be used to keep food warm—and without the fear of burning it—once it has been reheated on the stove or in the oven.

One of the other concerns about food safety and the slow cooker is if there is a loss of power in the house—especially if you don't know when it occurred in the cooking process. If you're home, and the amount of time was minimal, add it back into your end time. If the time without power increases to more than 30 minutes, finish the food by conventional cooking, adding more liquid, if necessary.

However, if you set the slow cooker before you left for work, and realize from electric clocks that power was off for more than an hour, it's best to discard the food, even if it looks done. You have no idea if the power outage occurred before the food passed through the "danger zone." Better safe than sorry.

> Always thaw food before placing it in the slow cooker to ensure the trip from 40°F to 140°F is accomplished quickly and efficiently. While adding a package of frozen green beans will slow up the cooking, starting with a frozen pot roast or chicken breast will make it impossible for the Low temperature of the slow cooker to accomplish this task.

Slow Cooker Hints

Slow cookers can be perplexing if you're not accustomed to using one. Here are some general tips to help you master slow cooker conundrums:

✳ Remember that cooking times are wide approximations—within hours rather than minutes! That's because the age or power of a slow cooker as well as the temperature of ingredients must be taken into account. Check the food at the beginning of the stated cooking time, and then gauge whether it needs more time and about how much time. If carrots or cubes of potato are still rock-hard, for example, turn the heat to High if cooking on Low, and realize that you're looking at another hour or so.

✳ Foods cook faster on the bottom of a slow cooker than at the top because there are more heat coils and they are totally immersed in the simmering liquid.

✳ Appliance manufacturers say that slow cookers can be left on either High or Low unattended, but use your own judgment. If you're going to be out of the house all day, it's advisable to cook food on Low. If, on the other hand, you're going to be gone for just a few hours, the food will be safe on High.

✳ Use leaf versions of dried herbs such as thyme and rosemary rather than ground versions. Ground herbs tend to lose potency during many hours in the slow cooker.

✳ If you want a sauce to have a more intense flavor, you can reduce the liquid in two ways. If cooking on Low, raise the heat to High, and remove the lid for the last hour of cooking. This will achieve some evaporation of the liquid. Or, remove the liquid either with a bulb baster or strain the liquid from the solids, and reduce them in a saucepan on the stove.

Slow Cooker Cautions

Slow cookers are benign, but they are electrical appliances with all the concomitant hazards of any machine plugged into a live wire. Be careful that the cord is not frayed in any way, and plug the slow cooker into an outlet that is not near the sink.

Here are some tips on how to handle them:

✳ Never leave a slow cooker plugged in when not in use. It's all too easy to accidentally turn it on and not notice until the crockery insert cracks from overheating with nothing in it.

✳ Conversely, do not preheat the empty insert while you're preparing the food because the insert could crack when you add the cold food.

✳ Never submerge the metal casing in water or fill it with water. The inside of the metal does occasionally get dirty, but you can clean it quite well with an abrasive cleaner and then wipe it with a damp cloth or paper towel. While it's not aesthetically pleasing to see dirty metal, food never touches it, so if there are a few drips here and there it's not really important.

✳ Always remember that the insert is fragile, so don't drop it. Also, don't put a hot insert on a cold counter; that could cause it to break, too. The reverse is also true. While you can use the insert as a casserole in a conventional oven (assuming the lid is glass and not plastic), it cannot be put into a preheated oven if chilled.

✳ Resist the temptation to look and stir. Every time you take the lid off the slow cooker, you need to add 10 minutes of cooking time if cooking on High and 20 minutes if cooking on Low to compensate. Certain recipes in this book instruct you to add ingredients during the cooking time. In those cases the heat loss from opening the pot has been factored in to the total cooking time.

✳ Don't add more liquid to a slow cooker recipe than that specified in the recipe. Even if the food is not submerged in liquid when you start, foods such as meats and vegetables give off liquid as they cook; in the slow cooker, that additional liquid does not evaporate.

Modern slow cookers heat slightly hotter than those made thirty years ago; the Low setting on a slow cooker is about 200°F while the High setting is close to 300°F. If you have a vintage appliance, it's a good idea to test it to make sure it still has the power to heat food sufficiently. Leave 2 quarts water at room temperature overnight, and then pour the water into the slow cooker in the morning. Heat it on Low for 8 hours. The temperature should be 185°F after 8 hours. Use an instant read thermometer to judge it. If it is lower, any food you cook in this cooker might not pass through the danger zone rapidly enough.

High-Altitude Adjustment

Rules for slow cooking, along with all other modes of cooking, change when the slow cooker is located more than 3,000 feet above sea level. At high altitudes the air is thinner so water boils at a lower temperature and comes to a boil more quickly. The rule is to always cook on High when above 3,000 feet; use the Low setting as a Keep Warm setting.

Other compensations are to reduce the liquid in a recipe by a few tablespoons and add about 5 to 10 percent more cooking time. The liquid may be bubbling, but it's not 212°F at first.

Converting Recipes for the Slow Cooker

Once you feel comfortable with your slow cooker, you'll probably want to use it to prepare your favorite recipes you now cook on the stove or in the oven. The best recipes to convert are "wet" ones with a lot of liquid, such as stews, soups, chilies, and other braised foods. Not all dishes can be easily converted to slow cooked dishes. Even if a dish calls for liquid, if it's supposed to be cooked or baked uncovered, chances are it will not be successfully transformed to a slow cooker recipe, because the food will not brown and the liquid will not evaporate.

The easiest way to convert your recipes is to find a similar one in this book and use its cooking time for guidance. When looking for a similar recipe, take into account the amount of liquid specified as well as the quantity of food. The liquid transfers the heat from the walls of the insert into the food itself, and the liquid heats in direct proportion to its measure.

You should look for similar recipes as well as keep in mind some general guidelines:

✳ Most any stew or roast takes 8 to 12 hours on Low and 4 to 6 hours on High.

✳ Chicken dishes cook more rapidly. Count on 6 to 8 hours on Low and 3 to 4 hours on High.

✳ Quadruple the time from conventional cooking to cooking on Low, and at least double it for cooking on High.

✳ Cut back on the amount of liquid used in stews and other braised dishes by about half. Unlike cooking on the stove or in the oven, there is little to no evaporation in the slow cooker.

✳ For soups, cut back on the liquid by one-third if the soup is supposed to simmer uncovered, and cut back by one-fourth if the soup is simmered covered. Even when covered, a soup that is simmering on the stove has more evaporation than one cooked in the slow cooker.

Chapter 2

Breakfast Treats and Heartier Eats

*P*reparations for Christmas and other holidays can make for very busy days. You may feel like getting out the door as soon as possible in the morning is going to be more beneficial to your to-do list than lingering over breakfast—and you may be right! With the slow cooker, you can be sure to have a fresh, healthy breakfast ready when you wake up.

Slow cooker breakfasts aren't all about convenience, either. The meals they yield are also great for lazy mornings of lounging around, watching the snow fall, or double-checking your gift lists. They'll save the day when you are descended upon by extra family or friends, because you can make large breakfast casseroles that stay warm and moist while you're busy in the kitchen with other things.

Bed-and-Breakfast Oatmeal

When you prepare this the night before for a house full of guests, everyone can help themselves as they get up. How great is that?

Makes 8 servings.

8 cups water

2 cups steel-cut oats (do not substitute rolled or quick-cooking oats)

¼ teaspoon salt, or to taste

1. Combine water, oats, and salt in a 5- or 6-quart slow cooker. Turn heat to Low. Put the lid on and cook until the oats are tender and the porridge is creamy, 7 to 8 hours.

2. Sweeten with a moderate amount of brown sugar or maple syrup, and add milk or cream if desired.

Variations:

❋ Add ⅓ to ½ cup of a dried fruit of your choice (such as cranberries, cherries, apricots, or raspberries) at start of recipe and cook with the oats for 7 to 8 hours as directed.

❋ Add a cup or so of fresh, chopped fruit to the oatmeal when it's ready to be eaten. The best apple varieties are Fuji, Red Delicious, or Gala. Or combine with a Bosc pear.

Steel-cut oats are different from the rolled oats that are typically used to make oatmeal. Rather than a flattened kernel (that has sometimes also been pre-cooked, as for instant oatmeal), steel-cut oats are the inner portion of the oat kernel, cut into two or three pieces by steel blades—thus, the name steel cut oats. They take longer to cook and yield a thick, rich porridge—perfect for the slow cooker!

Eggnog-Cranberry Oatmeal

Here's a delightful way to sneak eggnog into a breakfast dish! Allow yourself the treat by telling yourself the cranberries add a bit of health food to this decadent hot cereal. Oh, and the steel-cut oats are, indeed, a great source of vitamins and fiber.

Makes 4 servings.

2 cups water

2 cups eggnog

1 cup steel-cut oats (do not substitute rolled or quick-cooking oats)

¼ teaspoon salt, or to taste

½ cup dried cranberries

Nutmeg or cinnamon to garnish

1. Combine water, eggnog, oats, and salt in a 5- or 6-quart slow cooker. Turn heat to Low, and cook for 4 to 5 hours.

2. Add the dried cranberries and gently stir. Continue cooking on Low for another hour until the oats are tender and the porridge is creamy.

3. Serve with a sprinkle of nutmeg or cinnamon if desired.

> Delightful at breakfast, this dish also makes a great late-night snack. Double the recipe and save half (let cool before refrigerating, and keep in the fridge for up to 3 days). When ready to reheat, put the oatmeal in a microwave-safe bowl or in a saucepan with some extra eggnog to keep it moist while it heats up. Get really naughty and add a dollop of whipped cream!

Quick Quiche

This is slow-cooked breakfast in a bowl. The great thing is that you don't have to stand over several skillets waiting for eggs and bacon to cook at the same time.

Makes 4 to 6 servings.

12 pieces bacon

1 tablespoon bacon grease

10 eggs, beaten

1 cup half-and-half

8 ounces shredded cheddar cheese

Salt and pepper to taste

Chopped fresh parsley (optional)

1. In a skillet over medium-high heat, cook bacon until crispy. Transfer cooked strips to a plate covered with a paper towel to absorb extra grease. When cool, crumble the bacon.

2. Use about 1 tablespoon of the excess grease to cover the bottom and sides of the slow cooker.

3. In a large bowl, combine the eggs, half-and-half, and shredded cheese. Season with salt and pepper. Pour the egg mixture into the slow cooker. Sprinkle the crumbled bacon on top. Cover and cook on Low for about 4 hours or on High for about 1½ hours. Don't let it cook too long, as it will dry out.

4. Serve by scooping out of the slow cooker. Garnish or sprinkle with parsley if desired.

Variations:
There are lots of things you can substitute for the bacon in this recipe, such as diced ham, or, for a meatless quiche, small florets of just-tender broccoli or 1 cup of baby spinach leaves. You can also swap in different kinds of cheeses.

Egg Casserole with Potatoes, Mushrooms, and Bacon

Potatoes, mushrooms, bacon, and rosemary make for great earthy flavors in this rib-sticking egg casserole.

Serves 10 to 12.

½ pound bacon

1 onion, chopped fine

1 cup sliced domestic mushrooms

4 large potatoes, peeled, washed, and cut into thin slices

1½ cups shredded Cheddar cheese

12 eggs

1 cup milk

½ teaspoon salt

½ teaspoon pepper

1 tablespoon chopped fresh parsley

1 teaspoon chopped fresh rosemary

1. Spray the inside of the slow cooker with nonstick cooking spray. In a large skillet, cook bacon until just done. Put cooked slices on a plate covered with a paper towel to cool and absorb excess fat. Drain all but about 2 tablespoons of fat from the pan. Add onion and mushrooms and cook until onions are translucent, about 5 minutes. Crumble the cooled bacon.

2. Place one-third of the sliced potatoes in the slow cooker. Sprinkle with approximately one-third of the bacon, then the onion/mushroom mix, and then about one-third of the grated cheese. Repeat layers, ending with the cheese.

3. In a large bowl, beat the eggs, milk, salt, and pepper until well mixed. Add the chopped parsley and rosemary, and stir to combine. Pour over the ingredients in the slow cooker, cover and turn on low. Cook on Low for 8 to 10 hours or on High for 3 to 5 hours, until casserole is set and eggs are thoroughly cooked. To test for doneness, insert a clean knife in the center. If it comes out clean, the eggs are set and potatoes are cooked.

With its long, slow cooking time, this is the perfect breakfast to prepare and get started before you head to bed so that it's ready for you in the morning. It's just the thing to keep you going during early-morning gift-shopping trips.

Three-Cheese Egg and Kielbasa Casserole

This breakfast recipe that is loaded with cheesy goodness to bring comfort on cold winter mornings.

Makes 4 to 6 servings.

14 slices whole grain sandwich bread

½ pound kielbasa, browned and drained twice to remove as much fat as possible

1 cup grated Monterey Jack cheese

1 cup grated cheddar cheese

½ cup grated mozzarella

12 eggs

2¼ cups milk

1 teaspoon salt

½ teaspoon pepper

¼ cup chopped fresh parsley

1. Spray the inside of the slow cooker with non-stick cooking spray.

2. Break up or cut bread into large squares. Layer bread, sausage, and cheeses until ingredients are used up.

3. Beat eggs, milk, salt, and pepper together. Pour egg mixture over the other ingredients. Cover and cook on Low for 8 to 12 hours or on High for 5 to 6 hours.

Variation:

Add zing to your morning by spicing up this dish. Add 1 teaspoon cayenne pepper, or substitute Pepper Jack for the Monterey Jack cheese. Add a few drops of hot sauce to the eggs before pouring over the other ingredients. You might even consider adding some sliced jalapeno peppers before cooking.

Cinnamon Bread Pudding

How sweet this is!

Makes 8 servings.

10 slices cinnamon-raisin bread,
cut into pieces, about 5 cups

14-ounce can sweetened condensed milk

1 cup water

1 teaspoon vanilla extract

4 eggs, beaten

Yogurt or crème fraiche

1. Spray the inside of the slow cooker with non-stick cooking spray. Place bread cubes inside.

2. Mix milk, water, vanilla, and eggs, and pour over the chunks of bread, gently stirring with a wooden spoon to coat the bread with the milk mixture. Cook on Low for 2½ to 3 hours.

3. Serve warm with a dollop of yogurt or crème fraiche.

Variations:

✻ To reduce the sweetness, you can substitute a thick bread like Challa or a thick-cut white bread for the cinnamon raisin bread. Add ¼ to ½ of a teaspoon of cinnamon to the milk mixture.

✻ For added flavor and texture, add a half-cup of dried currants.

Banana Bread

Moist and delicious, this tastes as great as it smells while it's cooking.

Makes 6 servings.

5 eggs, beaten

3½ cups milk

2 teaspoons vanilla

2 tablespoons ground cinnamon

½ teaspoon salt

6 cups plain breadcrumbs (or more to make mixture as thick as cooked oatmeal when mixed with all ingredients)

¾ cup packed brown sugar

1 tablespoon butter, melted

2 bananas, mashed or sliced

1. In a large bowl, mix all ingredients together until bread crumbs are thoroughly wet and mixture is smooth like thick oatmeal.

2. Spray the inside of the slow cooker with non-stick cooking spray, and pour the mixture inside. Cover and cook on Low for 7 to 8 hours or on High for 4 to 5 hours. For the last half hour of cooking, open the lid on one side and put the handle of a spoon under to keep the lid propped open. This will allow the moisture to escape. If you don't do this, you will have a layer of liquid all around the bread.

3. When the bread is done, a knife stuck in the middle will come out fairly clean. Serve warm.

Variation:
For an added taste treat, add a diced pear to the dough before cooking.

Because the dough for this bread is going in the slow cooker rather than in a loaf pan, it'll come out in a circle or oval depending on the shape of your cooker. It'll still taste amazing.

Fruity French Toast

Here's another delicious make-the-night-before option, as well as a great way to use bread that's on the verge of getting stale.

Makes 6 servings.

12 slices thick-cut bread (Challah is best)

6 eggs

1 teaspoon vanilla

1 teaspoon lemon zest

2 cups evaporated milk

2 tablespoons dark brown sugar

1 teaspoon cinnamon

¼ teaspoon nutmeg

2 cups diced fresh fruit, including apples, pears, bananas, raspberries, and blueberries

Non-stick cooking spray

1. Spray a 4-quart slow cooker with non-stick cooking spray. Layer the bread in the slow cooker.

2. In a small bowl, whisk the eggs, vanilla, zest, evaporated milk, brown sugar, cinnamon, and nutmeg. Pour over the bread. Cover and cook on Low for 6 to 8 hours.

3. Remove the lid, and cook uncovered for an additional 30 minutes or until the liquid has evaporated.

4. Divide up the bread and sauce, and garnish with fresh fruit.

> Be sure not to skip adding the lemon zest—it brings all the other flavors together.

Chapter 3

Holiday Punches, Grogs, and Nogs

*D*on't you love going to parties where there's a slow cooker of mulled wine? There are wineries that have these going throughout the holidays in their tasting rooms, and for good reason. When you come in out of the cold, a cup of mulled wine—or hot chocolate, or hot cider—will warm you to your core.

The slow cooker is your holiday friend for drinks, too, giving you the ability to slow-cook the ingredients until well blended, and then keep the drinks warm for the evening.

This chapter contains a variety of wonderful holiday libations for nights when you want to cozy up with family, friends, or even serve carolers as they come through. Consider a classic mulled wine, or make an outrageous hot chocolate, or inspire Santa's helpers with an Irish Cream Dream. A selection of festive mugs, a few nibbles, and you're good to go.

Holiday Grog

There's something about punch that makes a holiday gathering really special. Once prepared, keep it in the slow cooker and set the heat on Low.

Makes 8 to 10 servings.

12- to 14-oz package fresh cranberries

2 cups sugar

3 cups water

⅓ cup fresh-squeezed lemon juice

¾ cup fresh-squeezed orange juice

2 cinnamon sticks

1 or 2 cloves (optional)

1. Put the cranberries in a colander and rinse and sort them, discarding any that don't look good.

2. Put the sugar in a bowl and add the water, stirring to combine and partially dissolve the sugar.

3. Put the cranberries, the sugar water, lemon juice, orange juice, cinnamon sticks, and clove or two in the slow cooker. Cover and cook on Low for 3 to 4 hours.

4. Before serving, pour the contents of the slow cooker into a large bowl. Put a fine-mesh colander over the slow cooker, and slowly pour the grog back into the slow cooker so that the skins and pulp from the cranberries are strained out.

5. Serve from the slow cooker with the setting on Low.

White Christmas Hot Chocolate

You can be dreaming of a white Christmas, or you can be creating your own white-themed holiday regardless of whether snow is in the forecast. With this rich, creamy, snow-white hot chocolate, you'll definitely set the stage.

Makes 10 to 12 servings.

4 cups heavy cream

12 cups milk (not skim)

24-oz package white chocolate chips

1 teaspoon vanilla extract

1 cup white peppermint schnapps (optional)

Mini marshmallows (for garnish)

1. Combine the heavy cream and milk in the slow cooker, then stir in the white chocolate chips. Cook on Low for 2 to 3 hours, stirring occasionally.

2. When nearly ready to serve, stir in the vanilla extract and the peppermint schnapps. Cook on Low for another 5 to 10 minutes until the liquid is heated through.

3. Serve by ladling into decorative mugs, and garnish with mini marshmallows.

Make a themed evening out of this one even if you live somewhere warm, and invite friends to come over and watch the 1954 classic *White Christmas*, starring Bing Crosby, Danny Kaye, and Rosemary Clooney. Make the White Christmas Hot Chocolate, and sing along!

Over the Top-olate Hot Chocolate

For those who love thick, dark chocolate, this warm drink is like a favorite truffle already melted in your mouth.

Makes 6 to 8 servings.

12 cups chocolate milk (the highest quality possible, as it will have the best flavor)

4 tablespoons unsweetened cocoa powder

12-oz bag semisweet or bittersweet chocolate chips

2 cups heavy cream

1 tablespoon sugar

1. Pour chocolate milk into the slow cooker. Stir in 3 tablespoons of unsweetened cocoa powder until well combined, then add the chocolate chips and stir again. Cook on Low for 2 to 3 hours, stirring occasionally.

2. To make chocolate whipped cream: In a large bowl, whip heavy cream with beaters until it starts to thicken. Add sugar and additional tablespoon of unsweetened cocoa powder. Beat until the whipped cream is stiff, about 5 minutes.

3. Serve hot chocolate in mugs, and top with dollops of chocolate whipped cream.

Merry Mocha

When this chocolate-coffee combo is when made with whole milk and slow cooked for hours, there's something sublime about it.

Makes 8 to 10 servings

12 cups whole milk

4 cups fresh brewed coffee

1 cup sugar (or to taste)

1 cup coffee liqueur (optional)

Whipped cream for topping

1. Combine milk and coffee in the slow cooker, and stir in the sugar until thoroughly dissolved. Cook on Low for 2 to 3 hours.

2. When ready to serve, stir in coffee liqueur if desired, and continue to cook for about 10 minutes until thoroughly heated through.

3. Serve in Irish coffee glasses, and top with whipped cream if desired.

This is a wonderful drink to have going in the slow cooker all day when it's really nasty out. Wait until later in the day to add the coffee liqueur, of course—unless you know you'll be house-bound all day. This is perfect for warming up the family—whether they have been sledding, ice-skating, shoveling, or just on a white-knuckled drive home from work on bad roads.

Christmas Cranberry Punch

The cranberry is a great complement to the citrus, keeping the drink from being overly sweet. Serve with gingerbread cookies for a festive treat.

Makes 8 to 10 servings.

8 cups water

4 cups cranberry juice

1 cup orange juice

4 tablespoons fresh-squeezed lemon juice

1 cup sugar

½ teaspoon ground cloves

1 teaspoon ground cinnamon, or
1 cinnamon stick

½ cup orange liqueur (optional)

Fresh cranberries or orange slices
for garnish

1. Put water, cranberry juice, orange juice, lemon juice, and sugar in the slow cooker. Stir together until sugar is dissolved.

2. Add cloves and cinnamon. Cook on Low for 2 to 3 hours.

3. When ready to serve, remove cinnamon stick, strain any solids, and stir in orange liqueur, if desired.

4. Ladle into mugs, and garnish with fresh cranberries or orange slices.

> The color of this punch is as beautiful as a Christmas tree ornament!

Celebration Cider

This is a great drink to have waiting for you when you come home with your Christmas tree. It appeals to everyone in the gathering, young and old, and can be easily "decorated" with personal favorites, just like the tree!

Makes 8 to 10 servings.

Two 32-ounce cartons apple cider

2 oranges, cut into eighths, peel on

2 lemons, cut into thin slices

4 cinnamon sticks

4 tablespoons unsalted butter, softened

2 tablespoons sugar

1 teaspoon cinnamon

2 cups fresh apples, cored and cut into bite-sized pieces

2 cups fresh cranberries

2 cups fresh pears, cored and cut into bite-sized pieces

1. Pour cider into slow cooker. Add orange and lemon pieces, and stir. Add cinnamon sticks. Cook on Low for 3 to 4 hours.

2. While cider brews, in a small bowl combine softened butter, sugar, and cinnamon. Stir until well combined, and put in the refrigerator to harden.

3. When ready to serve, remove orange pieces, lemon slices, and cinnamon sticks. Ladle into mugs, and let everyone gathered add desired fruits. Top with a small spoonful of cinnamon-sugar butter, and stir.

Citrusy Cider

The delicious drink is suffused with lemon, which is a great pick-me-up on when you feel a cold coming on.

Makes 8 to 10 servings.

32-ounce carton apple cider

32-ounce carton lemonade

2 oranges, cut into thin slices

4 lemons, cut into thin slices

1 cinnamon stick

1. Pour cider and lemonade into slow cooker. Add orange and slices from 3 lemons, and stir. Add cinnamon stick. Cook on Low for 3 to 4 hours.

2. When ready to serve, remove cinnamon stick. Put one or two super-thin lemon slices into tea cups, and ladle the hot cider over the lemon slices.

Add an ounce of bourbon to almost replicate a hot toddy, which was often prescribed to relieve head colds.

Cranberry Pear Cider

This cider blend is less sweet than a more traditional apple cider, and the cranberries add a refreshing tartness. When the flavors have a chance to meld during the slow cooking, the result is a rich, earthy brew.

Makes 4 to 6 servings.

12 cups pear cider

4 cups cranberry juice cocktail (highest quality)

Sections from 2 oranges, peeled and all peel and pith removed

1 cup cranberries, rinsed and picked over

½ teaspoon cinnamon

Shot of hot cinnamon schnapps, optional

1. Combine pear cider and cranberry juice in the slow cooker. Stir, and add orange segments, cranberries, and cinnamon. Cook on Low for 3 to 4 hours, stirring occasionally.

2. When ready to serve, remove orange segments, and scoop out cooked cranberries with a slotted spoon.

3. Ladle into mugs, and add a shot of hot cinnamon schnapps if desired.

Pears have great symbolism—perfect for New Year's celebrations. In China, pears have represented immortality because pear trees live for a long time. In Korea, the pear symbolizes grace and nobility. In the novel *Their Eyes Were Watching God* by Zora Neale Hurston, the pear tree symbolizes inner peace.

Hot Buttered Rum

Now this is what Santa really wants when he makes it down the chimney! A totally decadent drink, this is one to serve by the fire on a night when a snowstorm is blowing outside—or when the kids are finally asleep.

Makes 6 to 8 servings.

16 cups warm water

4 cups dark brown sugar

1 cup unsalted butter, cut into pieces

1 teaspoon salt

4 cinnamon sticks

8 whole cloves

1 teaspoon nutmeg

1 cup dark rum (or to taste)

Eggnog for topping

1. Pour water into the crock pot. Add the brown sugar and stir until thoroughly combined. Stir in butter, salt, cinnamon sticks, cloves, and nutmeg. Cook on Low for 3 to 4 hours, or until the butter has melted and the mixture is quite hot.

2. When ready to serve, stir in the dark rum. Ladle into mugs, and top with eggnog if desired.

Steamy White Russians

A classic White Russian is two parts vodka to one part coffee liqueur, topped with cream, and sometimes served over ice. In cold, dark, dreary December, on a night when you need to wrap gifts for your coworkers, the slow-cooked, steamy version of this cocktail will revive your Christmas spirit.

Makes 4 to 6 servings.

2 cups heavy cream

6 cups milk (not skim)

¼ teaspoon vanilla extract

½ cup coffee liqueur

1 cup vodka

1. Combine cream, milk, and vanilla in the slow cooker. Cook on Low for 1½ to 2 hours.

2. When ready to serve, add coffee liqueur and vodka. Stir, heat through, and ladle into mugs.

The white Russian is a cocktail that's been around for a while, but wasn't as popular as it is today until the film *The Big Lebowski* gained a cult following. The Coen Brothers movie, which came out in 1998 and has gained such a cult following that there is an annual Lebowski Fest, stars Jeff Bridges as "the Dude." What's his favorite drink? A white Russian. Would he like it steamy? Without a doubt.

Mulled Wine

Fruits were popular gifts for the holidays in the olden days, when finding fresh fruit was often difficult, and when citrus fruit was a delightful change to dreary winter eating. Mulled wines are rich with fruits reflecting these gifts.

Makes 4 to 6 servings.

750-ml bottle dry red wine
1 orange, cut into thin wedges
1 lemon, juiced, seeds removed
¼ cup brandy
6 cloves
¼ cup honey
2 cinnamon sticks
2 teaspoons ground ginger

Put wine into slow cooker. Add orange wedges, lemon juice, brandy, cloves, honey, cinnamon, and ginger. Cook on Low for 1 to 2 hours. When ready to serve, remove orange wedges and cinnamon sticks. Ladle into mugs.

Variation:
Not a fan of cloves? Omit the cloves, use the juice of a second lemon, and, just before serving, add ¼ cup ginger liqueur (or 2 teaspoons ground ginger). The ginger liqueur adds an extra umph to the lovely blend. Makes 4 to 6 servings.

Egg-xotic Eggnog

Diet be damned. If Santa can stay jolly in his shape, we all might as well partake in some decadent holiday cheer.

Makes 8 to 10 servings.

Two 32-ounce cartons eggnog
2 teaspoons freshly grated nutmeg
6 egg whites
1 tablespoon sugar
1 cup dark rum

1. Put eggnog and nutmeg in the slow cooker. Cook on Low for 1 to 2 hours.

2. Put egg whites in large bowl and beat with electric beaters on high until soft peaks form, about 5 minutes. Add sugar and continue to beat until stiff, glossy peaks form. Set aside or refrigerate if you just started heating up the eggnog.

3. When ready to serve, add the rum and stir to combine and heat thoroughly. Ladle the eggnog into mugs. Top with a dollop of egg white "meringue" and dust with a sprinkling of fresh nutmeg.

In the 17th century, milk and eggs were sometimes scarce, and so a special cocktail featuring them was considered a luxury. It is even hypothesized that the Colonists called the drink "egg-and-grog," which became eggnog. It's been adapted around the world, and has become synonymous with Christmastime here in the United States.

Irish Cream Dream

When you're having a crowd for a holiday dinner and you're not sure what to make for dessert, get this going in the slow cooker, serve it to the adults, and bring out the Christmas cookies. Everyone will be thrilled!

Makes 4 to 6 servings.

6 cups strong-brewed black coffee

⅔ cup heavy whipping cream

2 tablespoons unsweetened cocoa powder

½ cup Irish Cream Liqueur

Whipped cream to garnish

1. Put coffee, heavy cream, and cocoa powder in the slow cooker. Stir to combine. Cook on Low for 3 hours, or until liquid is steaming.

2. Just before serving, add Irish Cream Liqueur and stir to combine. Ladle into mugs and top with whipped cream.

One of the best-known makers of Irish cream liqueur is Bailey's. Some interesting stats about Bailey production and distribution around the globe are that the ingredients are all sourced from Ireland. The cream alone is produced by 40,000 cows grazing on 1,500 farms along the Eastern Irish coast.

Chapter 4

Dips and Dishes for Nibbles and Noshing

For some of us, the appetizers are the best part of the meal. They're little bites of this and that—often the foods you'd otherwise pass on because they seem too rich, full of cheese and cream and spices. And while the appetizers can be decadent, there's justification in eating "light" by just nibbling on them. Hey, it's the holidays!

With meatballs, kabobs, wings, dips, and other tasty treats, this chapter was written with celebration, not deprivation, in mind. So indulge.

Merry Meatballs

Meatballs make every party special, so be sure to have them at the ready. While they should be cooked in the slow cooker, you can prepare the recipe, shape the meatballs, and put them in a single layer in a freezer bag and freeze until ready to finish in the slow cooker. No excuses for no meatballs!

Makes 4 to 6 servings.

2 tablespoon olive oil

1 small onion, finely chopped

3 cloves garlic, minced

½ teaspoon crushed red pepper flakes

1 large egg

2 tablespoon milk

½ cup Italian seasoned breadcrumbs

¼ cup grated Parmesan cheese

¼ cup grated mozzarella

2 tablespoon chopped fresh parsley

½ pound ground pork

½ pound ground chuck

¼ pound ground veal

Salt and pepper to taste

Prepared pasta sauce or home-made tomato sauce

1. In a large skillet over medium-high heat, combine oil, onion, and garlic. Cook, stirring, until onion is translucent, about 3 minutes. Add red pepper flakes and stir over heat for another minute.

2. In a large bowl, combine egg and milk and whisk together until well combined. Add breadcrumbs, Parmesan, mozzarella, and parsley. Mix well.

3. Add the meats and onion/garlic mixture to the bowl, and stir until combined, but don't overmix. Using your hands, form meat into 1½-inch sized balls and arrange in the slow cooker. Layer the meatballs if there isn't room for all of them on the bottom. Sprinkle with salt and pepper. Cover and cook on Low for 5 to 6 hours or on High for 3 to 4 hours, or until meatballs are cooked through.

4. Transfer the meatballs to a bowl with a slotted spoon. Drain fat from slow cooker. Heat the pasta sauce in a saucepan, then put it in the cooker. Return the cooked meatballs to the pot, cover, and keep on warm to serve.

Variation:
Make more meatball merriment by making smaller "mini" meatballs— about half the size of a normal meatball. The minis will cook more quickly, too, so be sure to cut the cooking time: Low for about 4 hours or High for about 2 hours.

Hot Dog and Bacon Bites

These are fun to make for any kind of party, but you can count on them being very well received over the holidays. They are also great after-school snacks for hungry teenagers. The best hot dogs are those made from grass-fed meat.

Makes 10 to 12 party servings.

2 pounds all-beef hot dogs
1 pound thick-cut bacon
Honey to drizzle

1. Slice hot dogs in half crosswise. Separate the bacon slices and cut them in half crosswise, as well. Wrap each hot dog half with a bacon strip, and fasten with toothpicks at the top and bottom.

2. Layer the wrapped hot dogs in the slow cooker, drizzling each layer lightly with honey. Repeat layers until hot dogs run out.

3. Cover and cook on Low for 2 to 3 hours. Remove with tongs, slice into bite-sized pieces, and put a toothpick into every piece to secure the bacon and make for easy eating.

Variation:
For thicker bites, replace the hot dogs with kielbasa. You'll need to cut the sausage into 3- to 4-inch pieces as well as slicing it in half crosswise.

Chicken Bites

You will be delighted by these seasoned chicken bites—so much healthier than the frozen nuggets so common in our fast-food cuisine. Play with the seasoning to make the sweeter or spicier.

Makes 6 to 8 party servings.

1 pound boneless skinless chicken breast or thigh

¼ cup olive oil

1 teaspoon fresh parsley, minced

2 garlic cloves, minced

1 teaspoon lemon zest

1 teaspoon onion powder

½ teaspoon cayenne

¼ teaspoon salt

¼ teaspoon pepper

1. If the chicken breasts are particularly thick, place them between sheets of waxed paper and pound them to about ½-inch thickness with a mallet or rolling pin. Cut the chicken into "nugget" sizes.

2. In a large bowl, combine olive oil with parsley, garlic, zest, onion powder, cayenne, salt, and pepper. Stir or whisk to combine well.

3. Put the chicken pieces in the bowl, and stir to coat. If desired, the chicken can marinate in the oil for up to 30 minutes in the refrigerator, but this isn't necessary.

4. Place the chicken in the slow cooker with the additional oil mixture. Cover and cook on Low for 4 to 6 hours or on High for 2 to 3 hours. In the last half hour of cooking, prop open the lid with the handle of a wooden spoon so some steam is released and the nuggets dry a little.

Serve these with toothpicks so they can be eaten easily—or dipped into a sauce. Try a spicy mustard, sweet-and-sour, or a barbeque sauce (or all three!). You could also keep them light and fresh by simply squeezing fresh lemon over them and sprinkling with chopped fresh parsley.

Curried Cauliflower

Really easy to make and really tasty! Vary the amounts of the spices if you lean more toward the flavor of one over another.

Makes about 3 cups.

1 head cauliflower

Olive oil for drizzling

Ground cumin

Ground turmeric

Ground cayenne

Ground coriander

Salt and pepper to taste

1. Core the cauliflower and break the head up into florets. You can trim and cut the stems into bite-sized pieces, as well.

2. Put the pieces into the slow cooker. Drizzle with olive oil so that there is a light coating of oil on the cauliflower. Lightly dust the oiled cauliflower with the spices, just so the florets and stems are covered. If you are a hesitant cook who isn't sure about quantities, you can combine about ¼ cup olive oil with 2 teaspoons curry powder—which is a pre-combined blend of the spices listed above—and pour this over the cauliflower.

3. Cover and cook on Low for 4 to 5 hours, or on High for 2 to 3 hours until the cauliflower is tender. Season with salt and pepper, and serve in a bowl that has been lined with fresh lettuce leaves.

Variation:

For a more colorful dish, replace half of the head of cauliflower with half a head of broccoli.

Santa's Spinach-Artichoke Dip

You can try this dip without the spinach if you want, but it adds color as well as flavor and a bit more moisture.

Makes 6 to 8 servings.

2 10-oz bags frozen spinach, thawed and squeezed dry

2 14-oz cans artichoke hearts packed in water, drained and chopped

8 oz cream cheese

1 cup shredded mozzarella

½ cup grated Parmesan

1 clove garlic, minced

¼ cup milk

Salt and pepper to taste

Non-stick cooking spray

1. Spray the inside of a large slow cooker with the cooking spray.

2. Combine all ingredients in a large bowl, and transfer to the slow cooker. Cover and cook on Low for 2 to 3 hours, or on High for 1 to 2 hours, or until all cheese is melted.

Colorful crudités to serve with this include baby carrots, strips of red and yellow bell pepper, celery, endives, and fennel. You might even entice Santa to take up vegetables if you leave his favorite dip rather than cookies and milk.

Devils on Horseback

Here's a slow-cooker take on the classic cocktail party food of the 1970s, which is still very popular today. Be sure to crack the lid on the slow cooker as directed so the bacon gets a bit crispy.

Makes 24.

24 large dates, pitted

12 slices thick-cut bacon, halved

Toothpicks

1. Wrap each date in a piece of bacon and secure with a toothpick.

2. Place the "devils" in the slow cooker. Their sides can touch. Cover and cook on High for 2 to 3 hours. During the last hour, prop the lid open with the handle of a wooden spoon. This allows the steam to escape and makes the snacks crispier. Serve hot.

Variation:

If you want an extra layer of flavor, consider drizzling the wraps with a tiny bit of honey—just enough for a drop or two per wrap. You can also sprinkle them lightly with cayenne or curry powder during the last hour of cooking when the lid is ajar for an extra zing.

Nutty Honey-Mustard Wings

This is a great non-traditional sauce in which to cook chicken wings, giving them a savory yet sweet taste sensation.

Makes 6 to 10 servings.

4 pounds chicken wings

Salt and pepper

1 cup Dijon mustard

⅔ cup honey

½ cup sesame oil

½ cup chopped fresh cilantro

1. Preheat oven to 400 degrees F. Rinse the chicken wings with cold water, and cut off any excess skin. Line a cookie sheet with foil, put the wings on it, and put them in the oven, turning to cook them for about 5 minutes a side. Put the wings in the slow cooker. Sprinkle with salt and pepper.

2. In a bowl, combine the mustard, honey, sesame oil, and cilantro. Whisk to combine thoroughly.

3. Pour the sauce over the wings. Cover and cook on Low for 4 to 6 hours or on High for 3 to 4 hours. For the last half hour, prop the lid open with the handle of a wooden spoon to allow some steam to escape and liquid to evaporate.

4. Transfer wings to a serving dish with a slotted spoon. Remove as much fat as possible from the sauce, and serve some for dipping on the side.

Variation:

Enhance the nuttiness of the sauce by toasting some sesame seeds and sprinkling them over the wings before serving.

Kris Kringle Kabobs

Traditional Christmas colors of red and green make these slow cooker kabobs especially festive. They're easy and fun to make, and the kids can help, too.

Makes 8 to 10 servings.

1 pound chicken cutlets, excess skin removed and cut into bite-sized pieces

2 green bell peppers, cored, seeded, and cut into bite-sized pieces

2 red bell peppers, cored, seeded, and cut into bite-sized pieces

½ fresh lemon, seeds removed

1 cup Italian dressing

2 cloves garlic, crushed

Salt and pepper to taste

Bamboo skewers

1. Break the skewers in half so the 4-inch segments can fit in the slow cooker. Remove anything resembling splinters on the ends.

2. Skewer the kabobs alternating chicken pieces and vegetables in whatever kind of pattern you want.

3. Put the kabobs in the slow cooker. Squeeze the juice from the lemon over the kabobs. Combine the Italian dressing with the crushed garlic, and pour over the kabobs.

4. Cover and cook on Low for 4 to 6 hours or on High for 3 to 4 hours or until chicken is cooked through and peppers are tender. Season with salt and pepper before serving.

Variation:
Sweet onions are another great addition to these kabobs. Use slices from wedges of Vidalia onions for the best flavor. Zucchini are another option.

Party Portobellos

There's nothing like a big slice of slow-cooked Portobello mushroom, when the flavor explodes with every bite. This is another so simple but so satisfying recipe that can easily be doubled to make extra. You'll want to be able to quickly reheat them to enjoy through the week.

Makes about 2 cups cooked Portobellos.

3 large Portobello mushrooms, loose, or 16 to 18 oz package or Portobellos

3 tablespoons olive oil

3 tablespoon butter

Salt and pepper to taste

Chopped rosemary for garnish, if desired

1. Go over the Portobellos and remove any obvious dirt by brushing or shaking it off. Slice the Portobellos into thick slices (¼-inch or so). Put the slices into the slow cooker.

2. In a small skillet, heat the olive oil and butter over medium heat until melted and combined. Pour the melted oil/butter combo over the Portobellos.

3. Cover and cook on Low for 3 to 4 hours or on High for 1 to 2 hours. The mushrooms should be cooked through but not too mushy. Season lightly with salt and pepper before serving, and if desired, garnish with rosemary in the serving dish. Have toothpicks available for serving these at a party.

The Portobello mushroom is an oversized crimini mushroom. Both are dark-brown mushrooms related to the common mushroom. Creminis and Portobellos share a mustier, earthier flavor as well as color from the common white mushroom. Large Portobellos are so meaty that they are often cooked as meat substitutes, making great "burgers" for vegetarians.

Crabby Dip

This will take the bah-humbug out of anyone who's had a long day in lines at the mall. Serve with a very cold beer.

Makes 6 to 8 servings.

8 ounces cream cheese

1 cup mayonnaise

2 teaspoon Old Bay seasoning

½ teaspoon dry mustard

1 pound lump crabmeat

¼ cup shredded cheddar cheese

Non-stick cooking spray

1. Spray slow cooker liberally with non-stick cooking spray.

2. In a large bowl, combine cream cheese, mayonnaise, Old Bay, and dry mustard. Mix thoroughly. Add crabmeat and cheddar, and stir to combine.

3. Transfer mixture to the slow cooker. Cover and cook on Low for 5 to 6 hours until bubbly and gooey. During the last 15 minutes of cooking, prop open the lid with the handle of a wooden spoon to allow moisture to escape.

Old Bay Seasoning was developed in the Chesapeake Bay area of Maryland in the late 1930s, and was bought by McCormick & Company in 1990. It is a proprietary blend of spices including mustard, paprika, celery salt, bay leaf, black pepper, crushed red pepper flakes, mace, cloves, and nutmeg. It's used to season crabs, primarily, but also things as varied as potato chips and Bloody Marys.

Spicy Black Bean Dip

Liven up a holiday party where it's cold outside by bringing this dip that features South-of-the-Border ingredients. Ole!

Makes 8 to 10 servings.

16-oz can refried beans

15-oz can black beans, drained and rinsed

1 small can sweet yellow corn

16-oz jar salsa (mild, medium, or hot, to your liking)

4-oz can diced jalapenos, drained of all but 2 teaspoons juice

2 cups shredded Cheddar cheese

Non-stick cooking spray

1. Spray the inside of the slow cooker liberally with the non-stick spray.

2. In a bowl, combine refried beans, black beans, corn, salsa, jalapenos and the 2 teaspoons of juice, and 1 cup of cheese. Stir, then transfer to the slow cooker.

3. Cover and cook on Low for 3 to 4 hours, stirring mid-way through cooking. When ready to serve, top with remaining cheese and cook for another 10 minutes, until melted.

Have fun with this sassy, South-of-the-Border dip by dressing it up for festive holiday parties. Put it in a Christmas-theme bowl, but decorate with Southwestern-theme plastic cactuses or a fiesta tabletop decoration.

Chapter 5

Holiday Soups and Stews

*T*he holidays really are a time to revel in cooking and baking. There are so many ways to celebrate with good food! If this is your year to make cookies for all the special people on your list, and you know you'll be busy baking, then start with this chapter on slow-cooker soups and stews. The easy preparation of these recipes will help set the mood for your time in the kitchen, and while you're up to your elbows in butter, sugar, and sprinkles, your soups and stews will be doing their thing without taking up room or time in or on the oven. Perfect!

Another wonderful thing about these recipes is that they are suitable for a crowd. Make them, serve them, and refrigerate or even freeze any leftovers you may have—or just be prepared when someone wants a late-night snack. Best of all, soup and stew is good food—nourishing and comforting, which is just what busy holiday cooks and bakers need.

Chicken Stock for Healthy Holidays

Besides being the base of so many recipes, homemade stock is in and of itself an amazing food. Made with all parts of the chicken (or beef, or fish), a slow-cooked stock is rich in many minerals essential to good health, including calcium, magnesium, phosphorous, silicon, sulphur, and even glucosamine and chondroitin, which we often pay a lot of money for as a supplement for joint care! It is prized around the world as a remedy for whatever ails you, from digestive upset to sore throats to low libido.

Makes about 20 cups or 15 to 18 servings.

1 whole free-range chicken, or 2 to 3 pounds of the bony parts (necks, backs, breastbones, legs, wings)

Gizzards from the chicken

2 to 4 chicken feet (optional but beneficial)

1 large onion, chopped

2 carrots, peeled and sliced

2 celery stalks, chopped

4 quarts cold water

2 tablespoons vinegar

1 bunch parsley, chopped

1. If you are using a whole chicken, cut off the neck, wings, and legs and cut them into pieces. Cut the rest of the chicken pieces into chunks.

2. Place chicken pieces in the slow cooker and top with all vegetables except the parsley. Cover with water and vinegar. Cover, and let the meat and vegetables sit in the liquid for 30 minutes to 1 hour.

3. Turn the slow cooker to High and cook for 2 to 3 hours, or until boiling. Remove the cover and spoon off and discard any scum that has risen to the top.

4. Replace the cover and reduce the heat to Low. Cook for 8 to 10 hours. Add the parsley in the last 15 minutes or so.

5. When cooking is complete, remove the solids with a slotted spoon into a colander over a bowl. Any drippings in the bowl can go back into the stock. Remove any meat from the bones and eat separately.

6. Transfer the stock to a large bowl and refrigerate. When the fat is congealed on top, remove it, and transfer the stock to several smaller containers with tight-fitting lids. Stock can be stored in the refrigerator for several days, or kept frozen.

Variation:
For a browner, even richer stock, place the chicken pieces on a cookie sheet. Preheat the oven broiler, and broil for about 3 minutes per side, until browned.

The amounts in this recipe are for a larger slow cooker; if yours is small, cut the recipe in half.

Hot and Sour Soup

This is such a yummy combination of hot and sour tastes!

Makes 4 to 6 servings.

3 pounds boneless pork chops

½ onion, chopped fine

4 cloves garlic, minced

14.5-oz can bamboo shoots, drained

1 can sliced water chestnuts, drained

2 tablespoons rice vinegar

1 teaspoon sesame seed oil

1 to 3 teaspoon hot chili oil, depending on how hot you like it

2 tablespoons lemon juice

2 tablespoons soy sauce

2 Portobello mushrooms, sliced

2 cups chicken stock or broth

1 cup water

1. Place the pork chops on the bottom of the slow cooker, and cover with the onions and garlic.

2. Next, layer the bamboo shoots and water chestnuts on top of the chops. In a 2-cup measuring cup or small bowl, combine the vinegar, sesame seed oil, chili oil, lemon juice, and soy sauce. Pour over the other ingredients in the slow cooker.

3. Add a layer of the Portobello mushrooms, and cover everything with the chicken stock and water. Cook on Low for 5 to 7 hours or on High for 3 to 4 hours.

My family loves the tanginess of the vinegar as a complement to the spiciness, so I am liberal with the lemon juice and the rice vinegar. Adjust the soup to your liking by adding to or using less of both the vinegar/lemon or the chili oil.

Back-for-More Beef Stew

Slow-cooked beef stew is such a treat. There's something about what happens to the vegetables when the fat and juices from the beef cook for hours alongside them that makes magic from these simple ingredients.

Makes 4 to 6 servings.

2 tablespoons olive oil or canola oil

1 onion, chopped fine

2 cloves garlic, minced

3 to 4 pounds chuck or bottom round beef

4 carrots, sliced

½ pound green beans, tops and bottoms snipped, and cut into 2-inch pieces

1 large potato, peeled and cubed

4 cups beef stock or broth

1 teaspoon arrowroot for thickener, if desired

1. Heat the oil in a skillet and add the onions and garlic, cooking over medium-high heat until the onion is translucent, about 3 to 5 minutes.

2. Put the beef in the slow cooker and cover with the onion/garlic mixture. Add carrots, beans, and potato, and pour beef broth over everything.

3. Cover and cook on Low for 6 to 8 hours or on High for 4 to 5 hours.

4. If you like a thicker sauce, when the stew is cooked, take out about a half cup of the juices and mix in the arrowroot. Pour back into the stew and stir to combine. Let sit for 10 to 15 minutes on warm before serving.

Curried Carrot Soup

If you can find high-quality Madras curry, you'll find it has a deeper flavor and a bit less heat than standard ground curry powder. No matter, you'll still have the great curry flavor.

Makes 6 to 8 servings.

2 tablespoons olive oil

2 medium onions, chopped

4 teaspoon curry powder

1 tablespoon fresh ginger, grated

3 pounds carrots, peeled and chopped

4 cups vegetable or chicken broth

5 cups water

Salt and pepper to taste

1. Heat the oil in a skillet and add the onions, cooking over medium-high heat until the onion is translucent, about 3 to 5 minutes. Turn the heat to low and add the curry powder and ginger, stirring constantly for about a minute.

2. Put the carrots in the slow cooker, and scrape the onion mixture in on top. Cover with the broth and water.

3. Cook on Low for 4 to 5 hours or on High for 2 to 3 hours. Use an immersion blender to puree the soup, or process by batches in a blender. Serve hot.

Variation:
Substitute butternut or acorn squash for the carrots in this recipe, and if you want to add some additional spice, add 1 teaspoon cayenne pepper.

Chicken with Stars

With stars being symbols of the season, this is a divine holiday soup on a cold day.

Makes 4 to 6 servings.

1 teaspoon olive oil

1 onion, diced

3 cloves garlic, minced

2 stalks celery, chopped

2 carrots, peeled and sliced

2 tablespoons fresh thyme

3 tablespoons fresh rosemary, stems removed and coarsely chopped

1 pound boneless skinless chicken breasts, cut into cubes

½ teaspoon black pepper

2 cups chicken stock or broth

½ pound pasta stars

1 tablespoon chopped parsley

1. In a large skillet or pot over medium-high heat add the oil, onion, garlic, celery, and carrots. Cook for two minutes. Add herbs and chicken, and continue to cook and stir so that the chicken pieces turn white on all sides.

2. Transfer mix to slow cooker and add pepper and broth. Cover and cook on Low for 5 to 6 hours or on High for 3 to 4 hours. In the last hour of cooking (on Low) or half-hour of cooking (on High), add the pasta stars.

3. Stir in the chopped parsley before serving.

Variations:
Substitute boneless, skinless turkey breast, or pork loin for the chicken in this soup.

This recipe is bursting with fresh rosemary, which has cleansing and rejuvenating properties. It was a favorite of Napolean Bonaparte, who wore it to battle and also sent it to his wife and true love, Josephine.

Spinach Lemon Soup

To bring out the best in this soup, you must use fresh lemons. They're great to have around during the holidays, anyway, as they have a way of brightening anything they're added to, whether it's as simple as a pitcher of water, or as rich as butter cookies. Their acidity brings this yummy soup alive.

Makes 4 to 6 servings.

1 pound baby spinach leaves
6 cups chicken stock
¾ cup jasmine rice (uncooked)
2 eggs, lightly beaten
1 lemon, cut in half, seeds removed
Salt and pepper to taste

1. Remove any overly long or woody stems from the spinach. Rinse and shake dry in a colander. Put spinach in the slow cooker. Add the chicken stock. Cover and cook on High for about 1 hour.

2. Add the rice and stir. Cover and cook on Low for 2½ hours.

3. In a bowl, whisk together the eggs until thoroughly combined. Take a serving spoon of the hot soup and put it into the bowl with the eggs, whisking the liquids together. When combined, add another large spoonful and do the same. After the third spoonful, combine the egg mixture in the slow cooker. Squeeze the lemon into the soup and stir. With the cover off and the heat on Low, cook an additional 15 to 30 minutes, stirring often.

4. When heated through and thick, puree to a desired consistency with an immersion blender. Serve hot.

Most store-bought packages of spinach are pre-washed. This is very convenient, but this isn't always the freshest spinach. If you can find fresh spinach, that's the best. Be sure to thoroughly wash and rinse it to remove any dirt or sand, and remove any coarse stems.

Mushroom Bisque

An earthy, rich, mushroom bisque—like this one laced with sherry—will get any evening off to a festive start, whether you're serving it at a more formal gathering, or sharing a bowl with a friend by the fire while writing Christmas cards.

Makes 4 servings.

2 cups of water, brought to a boil

1 cup dried wild mushrooms, like chanterelles or porcini

1 tablespoon olive oil

1 tablespoon butter

½ onion, diced fine

1 stalk celery, thinly sliced

2 pounds fresh mushrooms, such as button or shiitake

1 teaspoon fresh rosemary leaves, chopped

¼ cup sweet sherry

1 cup chicken broth or stock

1 teaspoon fresh tarragon leaves, chopped

1 cup milk

Salt and pepper to taste

1. Bring about 2 cups of water to a boil. Place dried mushrooms in a large glass bowl or measuring cup. Pour the boiling water over the mushrooms and set aside. Tap or gently rinse the dirt off the fresh mushrooms, cut into small pieces, and set aside.

2. Heat oil and butter in a large skillet over medium heat. Add onions and cook, stirring occasionally, until onions are translucent, about 3 minutes. Add the celery, fresh mushrooms, and rosemary, and continue to cook a couple of more minutes. Transfer the mixture to the slow cooker. Add the sherry and porcinis with the broth. Cover and cook on Low for 3 to 4 hours or on High for about 2 hours.

3. Using a standard or immersion blender, puree soup until smooth. If using a standard blender, puree in small batches to prevent spillage. Add tarragon and milk just before serving, and season with salt and pepper.

Creamy Broccoli Soup

This recipe makes a bright green soup that lets the flavor of the broccoli shine through. It's seasoned with just a hint of nutmeg, which makes for a lovely Christmas presentation in the bowl—the bright red spice on the rich green soup.

Makes 8 to 10 servings.

¼ cup butter

1 onion, minced

2 large heads of broccoli, trimmed of coarse stalk and cut into chunks (approximately 6 cups)

48 oz chicken stock or broth

1 cup heavy cream

1 teaspoon salt

½ teaspoon pepper

Pinch of nutmeg for garnish

1. In a skillet over medium-high heat, cook the onion in the butter until translucent, about 3 minutes. Transfer onion to the slow cooker.

2. Add the broccoli, then the chicken stock. Stir to combine. Cover and cook on Low for about 6 hours or on High for about 3 hours, until broccoli is tender and cooked through.

3. Puree the broccoli with an immersion blender or by processing in batches in a blender. Add the cream, salt, and pepper, stir, and keep the heat on until heated through.

4. Serve in holiday china and garnish with a hint of nutmeg.

We can thank the Italians for the cultivation of broccoli (*broccolo* in Italian). It is in Italy that the "flowering cabbage" became popular, especially in the Roman Empire. Fibrous and rich in Vitamin C, most Americans grow up hearing how healthy broccoli is for them. It's available nearly year-round in supermarkets, which is great for those of us who love it.

Asian Squash Soup

The distinctive flavors of Thailand—lemongrass, ginger, red curry paste, and lime—give this soup layers of flavor that delight with every spoonful.

Makes 4 to 6 servings.

1 tablespoon olive oil

2 onions, diced

2 stalks lemongrass

4 cloves garlic, minced

2 tablespoons minced fresh ginger

1 teaspoon peppercorns

1 tablespoon cumin

1 large butternut squash, peeled, seeds removed, and cut into cubes

6 cups chicken stock or broth

1 can coconut milk, with 2 tablespoons reserved

Zest and juice of 1 lime

4 oz red curry paste

1 cup chopped fresh cilantro

1. In a skillet over medium-high heat, melt the olive oil and add the onions. Cook until translucent, about 5 minutes.

2. Trim the lemongrass stalks and cut them in half lengthwise down the middle. Add these, the garlic, ginger, peppercorns, and cumin to the onions, and stir to heat through, about 1 minute.

3. Put the butternut squash in the slow cooker, and top with the onion and spice mix.

4. Combine the chicken stock and coconut milk, pour over the other ingredients in the slow cooker, cover, and cook on Low for 5 to 6 hours or on High for 2 to 3 hours.

5. Keeping the slow cooker on warm, remove lemongrass stalks and discard. Combine the 2 tablespoons of coconut milk with the red curry paste and add this to the soup, along with the lime juice and zest, stirring to combine.

6. Puree the soup using a hand-held blender or working in batches to puree in a blender, returning the pureed mix to the slow cooker to keep it warm. When ready to serve, ladle into bowls and garnish with fresh cilantro.

> **Lemongrass is native to India but is grown worldwide and is a common ingredient in the cuisines of Thailand and Vietnam. Besides being aromatic, it has numerous health benefits, including as a digestive aid, for flatulence, to boost the immune system, and as a detoxing agent for the liver, kidneys, and digestive organs.**

Beef Barley Soup

Barley is one of those flavors and fragrances for a cold winter's night. There's something so rich and earthy about it that is accentuated by the Brussels sprouts. Serve the soup with crusty French bread.

Makes 4 to 6 servings.

1 small onion, minced

2 tablespoons olive oil

1½ pounds lean beef stew meat, cubed

1½ cups fresh Brussels sprouts, trimmed and cut in half

⅔ cup uncooked barley

48 oz (6 cups) beef stock or broth

1 teaspoon salt

½ teaspoon pepper

28-oz can diced tomatoes

1. In a large skillet, cook onion in 1 tablespoon of the olive oil over medium-high heat until onion is translucent, about 3 minutes. Add another tablespoon of oil, and add the beef. Stir so that all sides of the beef cubes get browned, about 5 minutes. Transfer the mixture to the slow cooker.

2. Add the barley, stock, salt, pepper, and diced tomatoes. Stir to combine. Cover and cook on Low for 6 to 8 hours, or on High for 4 to 5 hours until everything is tender and the barley is cooked through.

Barley is a grass, like wheat. It is one of the first domesticated grains and was long of great importance to our ancestors. The Ancient Egyptians used it to make bread and beer—uses that continue today. It is a whole grain, retaining its bran and germ after the hull is removed. Still a staple in the diets of many from the Middle East, barley is high in many essential nutrients, including phosphorous, magnesium, Vitamin B6, and calcium.

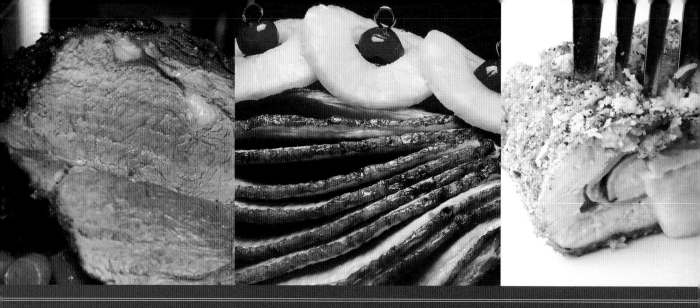

Chapter 6

Main Dishes with Meat

*E*ven the Whos in Whoville celebrated Christmas with a Roast Beast, as made famous in the Dr. Seuss classic *How the Grinch Stole Christmas*. Back in the days when meat was a luxury, to be able to serve a large roast for a gathering was indeed a very special treat. The tradition is as strong today, even though meat is more of a daily staple than a luxury for many of us. Everything becomes more special around the holidays, and the recipes selected here reflect that, including those for prime rib, rack of lamb, and even a version of beef Wellington.

As you gather at the table with family and friends for the holidays—whether it's around a roast beast or a pork loin—recall the Grinch and his story again in these last lines from the book: "Welcome, Christmas, bring your cheer. Cheer to all Whos far and near. Christmas Day is in our grasp, so long as we have hands to clasp. Christmas Day will always be just as long as we have we. Welcome Christmas while we stand, heart to heart, and hand in hand." Celebrate the season with good food and gratitude.

Short Ribs of Beef with Rosemary and Fennel

Short ribs are a wonderful cut because they become so meltingly tender when slowly braised in the slow cooker. The aromatic rosemary in the simple sauce cuts through the richness of the meat well.

Makes 4 to 6 servings.

5 pounds meaty short ribs with bones

¼ cup olive oil

1 large onion, minced

4 cloves garlic, sliced

2 cups beef stock or broth

1 large fennel bulb, cored, trimmed, and sliced

2 tablespoons fresh parsley, chopped

2 tablespoons fresh rosemary

2 teaspoons arrowroot (or cornstarch)

Salt and pepper to taste

1. Preheat the oven broiler, and line a broiler pan with heavy-duty aluminum foil. Broil short ribs for 3 to 4 minutes per side, or until browned. Arrange short ribs in the slow cooker, and pour in any juices that have collected in the pan.

2. Heat oil in a medium skillet over medium-high heat. Add onion and garlic, and cook, stirring frequently, for 3 minutes, or until onion is translucent. Scrape mixture into the slow cooker. Add stock, fennel, parsley, and rosemary to the slow cooker, and stir well.

3. Cook on Low for 8 to 10 hours or on High for 4 to 5 hours, or until short ribs are very tender. Remove as much grease as possible from the slow cooker with a soup ladle.

4. If cooking on Low, raise the heat to High. Mix arrowroot with 2 tablespoons cold water in a small cup. Stir this mixture into the cooker, and cook on High for 15 to 20 minutes, or until juices are bubbling and slightly thickened. Season with salt and pepper.

Our English word for beef comes from the Latin *bos*, which means "ox." By the Middle Ages, it had become *boef* or beef in English. There were cattle at the Jamestown settlement in Virginia in the early seventeenth century, but the Texas longhorns that we use for beef today were brought to that state by the Spanish almost a century after the Jamestown settlement.

Boeuf Bourguignon

Simple, elegant, and classic, this is the "stew" you make for special occasions. It's irresistible.

Makes 4 to 6 servings.

2 pounds stewing beef, fat trimmed, and cut into cubes

2 tablespoons olive oil

1 large onion, diced

3 cloves garlic, minced

½ pound white mushrooms, rinsed, stemmed, and sliced thick

1½ cups dry red wine

1 cup beef stock (use real stock for this; it adds a whole other dimension)

1 tablespoon tomato paste

1 teaspoon herbed de Provence

3 tablespoons fresh parsley, chopped

1 bay leaf

1½ tablespoons arrowroot (or cornstarch)

Salt and pepper to taste

1. Preheat the oven broiler, and line a broiler pan with heavy-duty aluminum foil. Broil beef cubes for 3 minutes per side, or until browned. Transfer cubes to the slow cooker, and pour in any juices that have collected in the pan.

2. Heat oil in a medium skillet over medium-high heat. Add onion, garlic, and mushrooms, and cook, stirring frequently, for 4 to 5 minutes, or until onion is translucent and mushrooms are soft. Scrape mixture into the slow cooker.

3. Add wine, stock, tomato paste, herbes de Provence, parsley, and bay leaf to the slow cooker, and stir well. Cook on Low for 8 to 10 hours or on High for 4 to 5 hours, or until beef is very tender.

4. If cooking on Low, raise the heat to High. Mix arrowroot (or cornstarch) with 2 tablespoons cold water in a small cup, and stir it into the slow cooker. Cook on High for 15 to 20 minutes, or until juices are bubbling and slightly thickened. Remove and discard bay leaf, and season to taste with salt and pepper. Garnish with some additional parsley if desired.

If you're not a wine drinker and making a recipe that calls for a small amount of wine, pour the rest of the bottle into ice cube trays and freeze it. When you need the wine for another recipe, simply pull out a few cubes and thaw.

Prime Rib

Yes, it is possible to make an amazing prime rib in the slow cooker! Searing the meat before it goes into the slow cooker is the key.

Makes 8 to 10 servings.

6- to 8-pound rib roast
4 tablespoons olive oil
Salt and pepper to taste
Meat thermometer

1. Trim excess fat from the roast.

2. In a large, heavy bottomed skillet, heat the oil until sizzling. Place the roast, fat side down, onto the oil and allow to cook until browned, 3 to 4 minutes. Turn the roast to the side and do the same, then flip it to brown the other side. Turn off the skillet.

3. Place the roast in the slow cooker. Season with generous sprinkling of freshly ground black pepper and kosher or sea salt. Cover and cook on Low for 6 hours.

4. Check the internal temperature of the meat by inserting the thermometer into a meaty section between some ribs. For medium, the temperature should read about 145 degrees F. If it's at that temperature or 5 to 10 degrees below, take it out of the slow cooker and let it rest on a warm plate. It can rest uncovered for 15 to 30 minutes.

> Isn't it a great feeling when you have done so little to prepare a dish, and yet it turns out so beautifully and is so delicious?

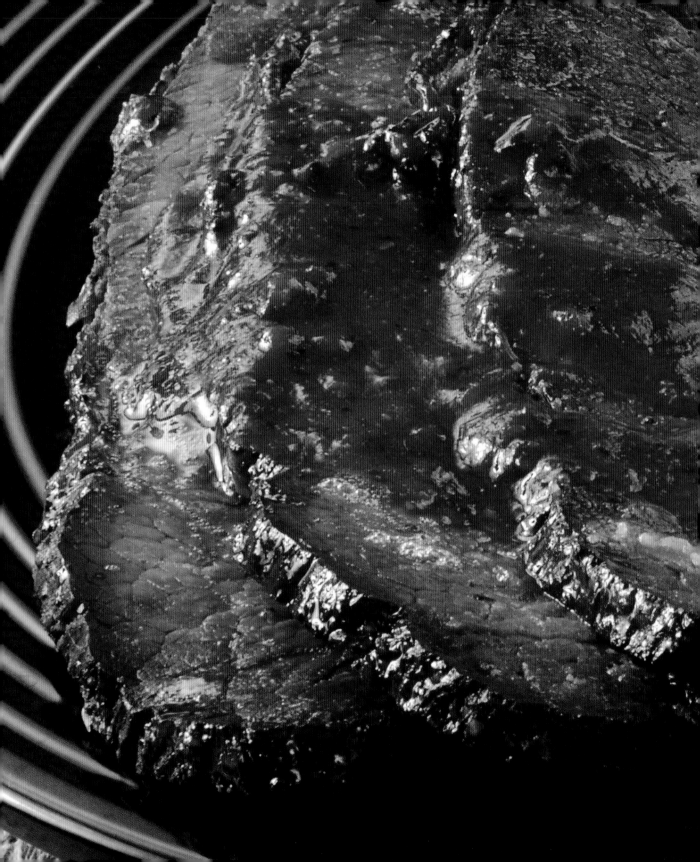

Spicy Brisket

Brisket is a great cut to put in the slow cooker, because it requires long, slow cooking to reach tender perfection. It's a great cut to serve over egg noodles, with the sauce on top. Temper the spices to your liking.

Makes 8 to 10 servings.

1 beef brisket, about 5 pounds
1 teaspoon salt
1 teaspoon sugar
1½ teaspoons cumin
1 teaspoon black pepper
½ teaspoon cayenne pepper
1 teaspoon ground coriander
½ teaspoon chipotle
4 tablespoons olive oil
2 onions, minced (about 2 cups)
4 cloves garlic, minced
2 tomatoes, cored, seeded and chopped
3 cups beef stock or broth

1. Bring brisket to room temperature. In a small bowl, combine salt, sugar, cumin, pepper, coriander, and chipotle. Use your hands to rub the spice mixture all over the brisket.

2. In a large skillet, heat 2 tablespoons of the oil over medium-high heat. When the oil is sizzling, sear the brisket in it, browning all sides (about 5 minutes per side). Transfer the brisket to the slow cooker.

3. Put the remaining 2 tablespoons of oil in the pan and cook the onions and garlic, stirring, for 3 to 5 minutes. Add this to the slow cooker. Top with the tomatoes and stock.

4. Cover and cook on Low for 8 to 10 hours or on High for 5 to 6 hours or until the brisket is fork-tender.

The brisket cut of beef is taken from the chest. It is one of the toughest cuts because of the connective tissue that runs through it. There are two versions—the flat cut, and the point cut. The flat cut is a bit more tender, but the point cut has more flavor because it is a bit fattier.

Easy and Elegant Tenderloin

This is a delicious cut of meat that deserves to shine on its own. A simple herb-based marinade adds just the right amount of flavor.

Makes 8 to 10 servings.

½ cup olive oil

1 tablespoon balsamic vinegar

1 teaspoon salt

½ teaspoon black pepper

½ teaspoon dried thyme

2 cloves garlic, pressed

1 bay leaf

5-pound piece of tenderloin, trimmed of excess fat

1. In a large bowl, combine the oil, vinegar, salt, pepper, thyme, garlic, and bay leaf. Add the tenderloin and turn to coat. Cover with plastic wrap and refrigerate for 2 to 3 hours.

2. Put the tenderloin in the slow cooker without the marinade. Cover and cook on Low for 5 to 6 hours, turning halfway through cooking.

As tender and delicious as this cut is, it can be complemented with a sauce when served, especially if potatoes are on the menu, too.

Horseradish sauce: 2 cups sour cream, ¼ cup prepared horseradish, 1 teaspoon of white vinegar, and salt and pepper to taste.

Mustard sauce: Sauté ½ cup shallots in 2 tablespoons of butter, add 1 cup of dry white wine, and stir in 2 tablespoons of Dijon mustard.

Simply Sensational Roast Chicken

The slow cooking yields tender, fragrant meat. If you want crisp skin, put the cooked chicken under the broiler in the oven for about 5 minutes. Chances are it won't matter to you when this is done.

Makes 4 to 6 servings.

1 onion, cut into thick slivers
1 carrot, sliced
4- to 5-pound whole chicken
1 lemon
1 teaspoon dried thyme
1 teaspoon dried sage
1 teaspoon sea salt
1 teaspoon ground black pepper
Optional: chopped fresh parsley

1. Place the slivers of onion and the sliced carrot in the slow cooker. Put the chicken on top of the vegetables. Squeeze the lemon over everything, then slice it into rounds and put a couple of the slices in the cavity of the bird. Season all over with thyme, sage, salt, and pepper.

2. Cover and cook on Low for 6 to 8 hours or on High for 3 to 4 hours. Season with additional salt and pepper, and chopped fresh parsley if desired.

> You could substitute an already-made blend of spices called Poultry Seasoning for the thyme and sage. The poultry blend contains those herbs, as well as marjoram, parsley, and sometimes savory and rosemary.

Turkey, Bacon, Cranberry Bliss

The saltiness of the bacon, the fruitiness of the cranberries, the slight gaminess of the turkey, and slow-cooked goodness. Delicious!

Makes 4 to 6 servings.

8 slices thick-cut bacon

1 boneless turkey breast, about 4 pounds

¼ teaspoon paprika

¼ teaspoon ground white pepper

2 Granny Smith apples, cored and cut into chunks

2 tablespoons dried cranberries

1. Put 4 or 5 slices of bacon on the bottom of the slow cooker, so that it covers the bottom.

2. Put the turkey breast on top of the bacon. Sprinkle with paprika and pepper. Add apples and cranberries. Layer the remaining slices of bacon over the mixture.

3. Cover and cook on Low for 8 to 10 hours or on High for 2 hours, then Low for 4 to 5 hours. The turkey will adhere to the bacon on the bottom, so you'll be able to pull off chunks of both. Transfer to a tray and serve.

Variations:

✳ Substitute dried currants, chopped dates, or dried prunes for the cranberries—or make a dried fruit mix with all of them.

✳ Try hot paprika instead of sweet, or add some chipotle for a smokier flavor.

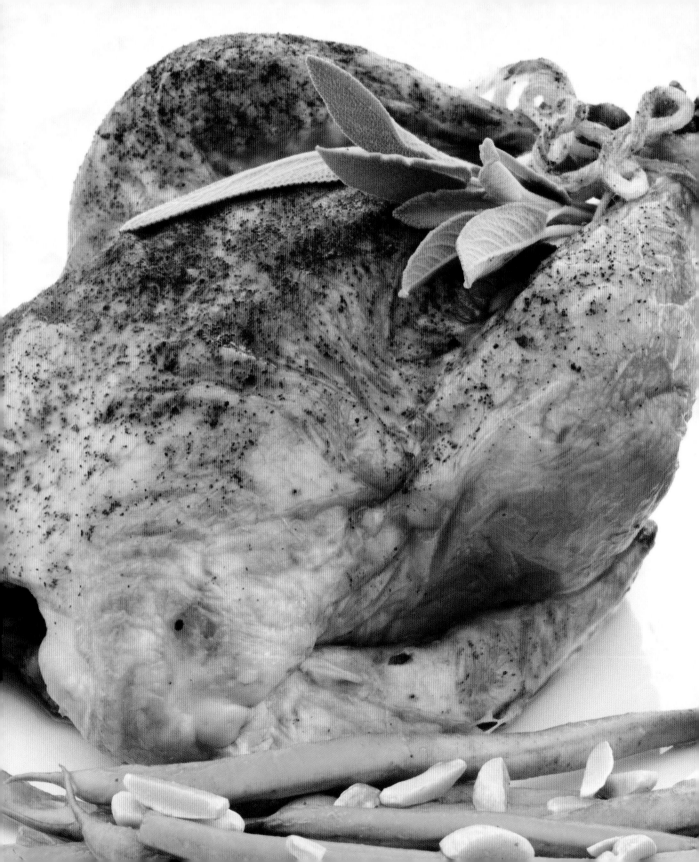

Cornish Hens with Fresh Greens

Cornish hens are as easy to make as dishes with chicken pieces, but there's something about them that makes the meal seem extra-special.

Makes 4 to 6 servings.

1 small onion, minced

1 garlic clove, minced

2 small Cornish game hens, split in two, skin removed

2 tablespoons olive oil

1 bunch Swiss chard, washed, coarse stems removed, and leaves chopped in large pieces

1 head Escarole, washed, trimmed, and chopped in large pieces

½ cup chicken stock or broth

1 pound baby spinach leaves

1. Heat oil in a small skillet over medium-high heat, and cook onions and garlic about 3 minutes, or until onion is translucent. Scrape mixture into slow cooker.

2. Place Cornish hens on top of onion mixture, breast side up, and top with Swiss chard, Escarole, and broth.

3. Cover the slow cooker and cook on Low for 6 to 8 hours or on High for about 4 hours, or until chicken is tender and cooked through. Add the baby spinach and cook for another 20 to 30 minutes. Season with salt and pepper.

The **Cornish Game hen** is a young, immature chicken, which is technically not supposed to be over 5 weeks of age or more than 2 pounds. It's the result of crossing the Cornish Game and Plymouth or White Rock chicken breeds.

Chicken Cordon Bleu

This dish is a decadent combination of ham and cheese stuffed inside chicken breasts, finished with a sauce of heavy cream.

Makes 4 to 6 servings.

6 medium-sized, skinless and boneless chicken breasts

1 pound Swiss cheese, cut into slices

1 pound cooked ham from the deli, sliced thin

3 tablespoons flour

1 teaspoon paprika

6 tablespoons butter

½ cup dry white wine

1 chicken bouillon cube

1 tablespoon arrowroot

1 cup heavy cream

½ cup chopped fresh parsley, for garnish

1. If your chicken breasts are thick, place them between sheets of wax paper and pound them to about ¼-inch thickness with a wooden mallet or rolling pin. Lay the breasts flat, and place slices of cheese and ham on them, distributing evenly. Fold breasts over and secure ends with toothpicks.

2. In a shallow soup bowl, combine flour and paprika and blend well. Dip chicken pieces in flour/spice mixture to coat on both sides.

3. Heat butter in a large skillet over medium-high heat, and cook the chicken pieces in the butter until browned on both sides, about 3 minutes a side. Transfer the chicken pieces with a slotted spoon to the slow cooker. In the butter and juices in the skillet, add the wine and bouillon cube and stir until cube is dissolved. Pour the mixture over the chicken in the slow cooker.

4. Cover and cook on Low for 5 to 7 hours or on High for 2 to 3 hours. Chicken should be cooked through and tender. Transfer chicken to a warm plate and cover with foil while you make the sauce.

5. Turn the slow cooker on High to heat the juices. In a measuring cup, mix the arrowroot and heavy cream until blended. Add a large spoonful of the hot juice to the cream mixture and stir, then pour the cream mixture into the slow cooker. Stir thoroughly and continue to stir while sauce thickens, about 5 minutes. Serve the sauce over the chicken.

The translation of cordon bleu is "blue ribbon," but this dish should not be confused with the prestigious French cooking school of the same name. In fact, the dish originated here in the United States in the late 1960s, and it was on the menu of the finest restaurants in the 1960s and 1970s. While there are many variations on the theme of a meat stuffed with cheese, other meats, or even seasoned butter, the closest variation appears to be the Swiss dish veal kiev, which is veal wrapped around ham and Gruyere cheese.

Holiday Ham

The whole family will love what the combination of the sweet and savory flavors do to the ham during slow cooking. For this recipe, be sure you're using a large slow cooker.

Makes 10 to 12 servings.

6- to 8-pound cooked, spiral-sliced ham

8-oz can crushed pineapple

½ cup honey

¼ cup firmly packed brown sugar

¼ cup Dijon mustard

Non-stick cooking spray

1. Spray the bottom of the slow cooker generously with non-stick cooking spray.

2. Place the ham flat-side down in the slow cooker. Pour the pineapple over the ham.

3. In a bowl, combine the honey, brown sugar, and mustard, and stir to thoroughly combine. Pour the sauce over the ham.

4. Cover and cook on Low for 6 to 8 hours or on High for 3 to 4 hours, finishing with a final 30 to 60 minutes on Low.

The history of the pineapple in America reveals why a pineapple-studded ham became a centerpiece of a holiday meal. Colonialists socialized quite a bit, and the ladies of the houses put together special centerpieces of fruit and vegetables on their dining room tables as a show of their wealth and status. The pineapple was the most special fruit one could include, and it was a must for any kind of special occasion.

Herbed Pork Roast

Pork is a best friend of garlic, and this recipe calls for plenty of it! Between that and the fresh herbs, by the time this dish is cooked, everyone's mouths will be watering from the aroma.

Makes 6 to 8 servings.

2-pound boneless pork roast

6 cloves garlic, minced

¼ cup fresh rosemary, chopped

2 tablespoons fresh parsley, chopped

2 tablespoons fresh sage, chopped

Salt and pepper to taste

3 ribs celery, cut into 4-inch lengths

⅓ cup chicken stock or broth

1. Rinse pork and pat dry with paper towels. Combine garlic, rosemary, parsley, sage, salt, and pepper in a mixing bowl. Make slits deep in the pork, and stuff half of mixture into the slits. Rub remaining mixture on the outside of the roast.

2. Arrange celery slices in the bottom of the slow cooker to form a bed for the meat.

3. Preheat the oven broiler, and line a broiler pan with heavy-duty aluminum foil. Broil pork for 3 minutes per side, until well browned. Transfer port to the slow cooker, and pour in any juices that have collected in the pan. Pour stock over pork.

4. Cover and cook on High for about 2 hours, then reduce heat to Low and cook for 4 hours, until pork is fork tender. Carve pork into slices and moisten with juices from the slow cooker.

> Browning meat under the broiler accomplishes two things when using a slow cooker. It gives the meat a more appealing color and it heats it so that it passes through the "danger zone" of 40F to 140F faster, especially if you're cooking on Low.

Apple-Stuffed Pork Chops

The trickiest part of pork chops is keeping them moist until they are thoroughly cooked. With the apple stuffing and the slow cooking, there's no need to worry—they will be succulent and delicious.

Makes 6 servings.

6 pork chops, bone in, cut thick (about ½ inch)

2 tablespoons butter

1 small onion, diced

2 celery sticks, diced

1 cup dried bread pieces

1 apple, peeled, cored and diced

1 egg, beaten

1 teaspoon fresh sage, chopped

½ teaspoon fresh thyme leaves

1 tablespoon fresh parsley, chopped

1 teaspoon lemon juice

Salt and pepper

⅔ cup chicken stock

3 carrots, diced

1 bay leaf

¼ cup chopped fresh parsley for garnish

1. Prepare the chops for the filling by using a sharp knife to create a pocket in the meat in the thickest part, extending the cut nearly to the bone.

2. Heat butter in a large skillet over medium-high heat and cook the onions and celery until translucent, about 5 minutes. Add the bread pieces, apple, egg, sage, thyme, parsley, lemon juice, and salt and pepper. Stir thoroughly.

3. In the slow cooker, add the chicken stock, carrots, and bay leaf and stir.

4. Stuff the chops with the apple mixture, distributing evenly, and position on top of carrots and broth in the slow cooker.

5. Cover and cook on Low for 8 to 10 hours, or on High for 5 to 6 hours until chops are tender. Season with salt and pepper to taste, and garnish with fresh parsley.

Variations:
You can get creative with the stuffing by adding dried fruit such as raisins or cranberries; crumbled sausage or bacon; or something spicy like hot pepper jelly.

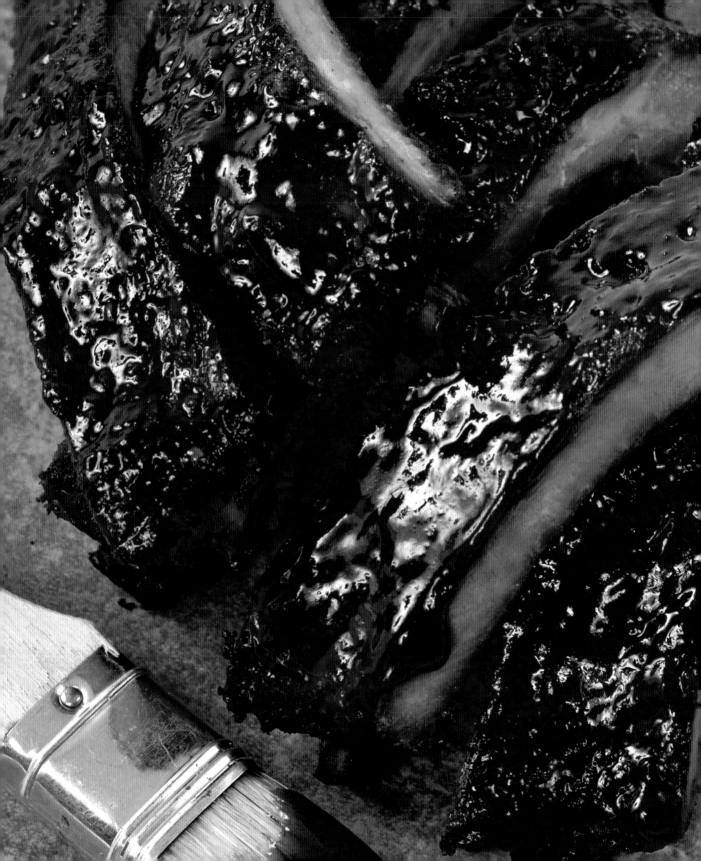

Christmas Ribs

Ribs can be so delicious, and are enjoyed by people of all ages. They may not be the fanciest thing to serve over the holidays, but they are guaranteed to make folks happy. They're great to come home to if you've been out caroling. Toss them on the grill to finish, and eat around the fire.

Makes 4 to 6 servings.

6 pounds pork spareribs

Cold water

2 cups ketchup

1 tablespoon Worcestershire sauce

¼ cup cider vinegar

1 teaspoon cayenne pepper

1 teaspoon chili powder

¼ teaspoon paprika

1 tablespoon brown sugar

1 clove garlic, crushed

Salt and pepper to taste

1. Cut ribs into chunks of 2 to 3 ribs each. Put into the slow cooker. Add cold water to cover the meat. Cover the slow cooker and cook on Low for about 8 hours or on High for about 5 hours. Transfer to a plate and allow to cool for about 30 minutes.

2. In a large bowl, combine ketchup, Worcestershire sauce, vinegar, cayenne, chili powder, paprika, brown sugar, and garlic. Stir to combine thoroughly.

3. Dunk ribs in the barbeque sauce and put on a platter. Grill the ribs for about 20 to 30 minutes over medium heat, applying more sauce as they cook. Pass the sauce when ready to eat.

Make the ribs the centerpiece of a holiday theme party featuring summer foods. Make potato salad, corn on the cob, baked beans, and whatever foods put you in the mood for summer. If you have a tree-trimming party on the same night, ask guests to bring an ornament that reminds them of summer.

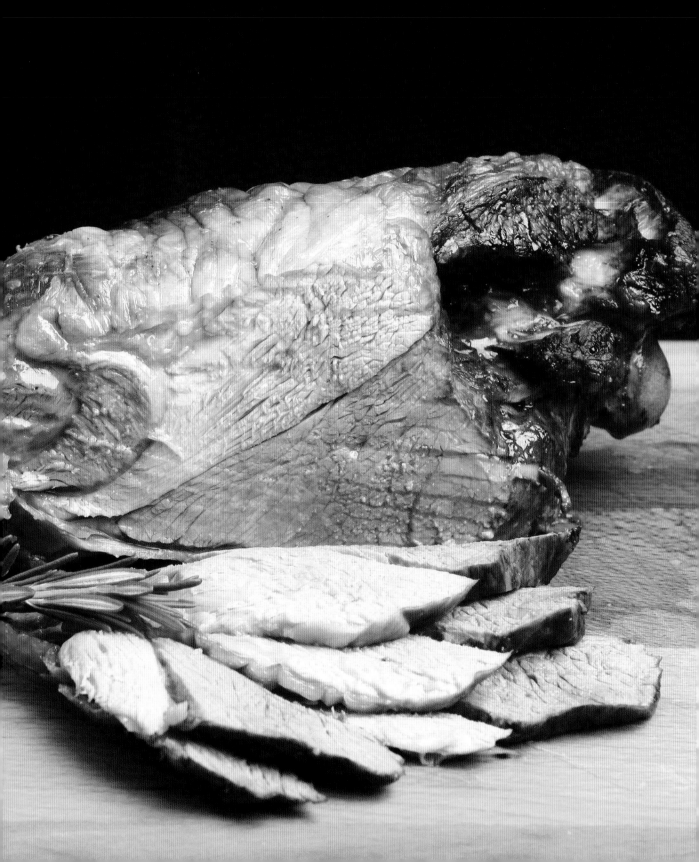

Lazy Lady's Leg of Lamb

Don't you just love the name of this recipe? You'll love the dish even more—promise! It's so delicious, and always comes out just right, with no fuss! Serve with mint jelly or your homemade mint sauce.

Makes 4 to 6 servings.

1 bone-in leg of lamb (shank removed)

1 tablespoon olive oil

½ teaspoon sea salt

½ teaspoon freshly ground black pepper

1 teaspoon fresh rosemary, chopped

1 teaspoon fresh mint, chopped

3 cloves garlic, minced

1. Put the olive oil in your hands and rub the oil all over the lamb.

2. Put the lamb in the slow cooker and sprinkle it all over with the salt, pepper, rosemary, mint, and garlic, rubbing the spices onto the meat.

3. Cover and cook on Low for 6 to 8 hours (do not cook on High).

4. Season with additional salt and pepper if desired.

Homemade Mint Sauce

1. On a cutting board, coarsely chop a large handful of fresh mint leaves (leaves removed from stems, washed, and dried). Put the mint in a glass container with a lid, like a Mason jar.

2. In a small bowl, whisk together 1 cup olive oil, 2 teaspoons white wine vinegar, 1 tablespoon fresh-squeezed lemon juice, 1 teaspoon honey, and ½ teaspoon salt. Pour over the mint leaves. Secure the lid and shake the mixture vigorously.

3. Refrigerate and let sit until ready to use. It'll keep for about a month.

Lamb Stew with Prosciutto and Bell Peppers

Lamb is an inherently rich meat, and the sweetness of red bell peppers combined with bits of salty prosciutto serve as perfect foils to that richness.

Makes 4 to 6 servings.

½ cup flour

2 pounds boneless lamb shoulder or leg of lamb, fat trimmed and cut into cubes

¼ cup olive oil

1 onion, diced

3 cloves garlic, minced

¼ pound prosciutto, cut into ½-inch chunks

1 cup dry red wine

1 cup beef stock or broth

2 tablespoons fresh rosemary, chopped

2 tablespoons fresh sage, chopped

2 tablespoons fresh parsley, chopped

1 large red bell pepper, seeds and ribs removed, thinly sliced

Salt and pepper to taste

1. Put flour in a large bowl and add meat, stirring to coat.

2. Heat oil in a large skillet and add meat pieces, shaking off excess flour as you transfer them from the bowl to the skillet. Brown the meat on all sides. Use a slotted spoon to put browned pieces in the slow cooker.

3. Add onion and garlic to the skillet and cook, stirring, for about 3 minutes. Scrape this onto the meat in the slow cooker.

4. Add wine to the skillet, and bring to a boil, stirring to dislodge the brown bits in the skillet. Pour mixture into the slow cooker. Add stock, rosemary, sage, and to the slow cooker, and stir well. Cook on Low for 6 to 8 hours or on High for 3 to 4 hours, or until lamb is almost tender.

5. If cooking on Low, raise heat to high. Add peppers, and cook for about an hour longer, or until lamb is tender. Season with salt and pepper.

This recipe calls for meat cut away from the bones, but by all means save those bones! Add them to your next batch of beef stock to make something with a bit more earthiness and depth.

Lovely Lamb Shanks

The shanks are less expensive, fattier cuts of lamb than the leg or shoulder. They are perfect for slow-cooking, though, like other cuts of meats that benefit from a longer cooking time to become juicy and tender.

Makes 4 servings.

4 to 5 pounds lamb shanks

½ teaspoon ground thyme

Salt and pepper

2 cloves garlic, sliced thin

½ cup dry red wine

½ cup beef stock or broth

15.5-oz can white beans

2 cups chicken stock

1 clove garlic, crushed

2 tablespoons olive oil

2 teaspoons white wine vinegar

Fresh thyme for garnish

1. Season the lamb shanks with the thyme, salt, and pepper. Place in the slow cooker. Cover with the garlic, red wine, and beef stock. Cook on Low for 8 to 10 hours or on High for about 6 hours.

2. In the last hour or so of cooking time, prepare a white bean puree. In a saucepan, crush the garlic into the chicken stock and cook over medium heat for about 5 minutes. Add the beans and continue cooking until beans are heated through. Puree with an immersion blender or by transferring to a blender. When smooth, add the olive oil and vinegar, and season with salt and pepper.

3. Put the puree on a serving platter with the lamb shanks on top. Garnish with the fresh thyme.

Americans eat far less lamb than people in many other countries, most notably New Zealand, Australia, the British Isles, Europe, and Muslim countries. What seems like a special meal for us because we eat it so infrequently is a common meal for people around the world—who eat proportionately less beef than we do.

Duck Confit

In essence, this is a simple dish of cured duck legs preserved in fat. It is considered a luxury, however, because it tends to be time consuming and most people aren't sure what to do with it once it's prepared. Here is a great, easy recipe. You will need to purchase the duck legs and fat at a specialty butcher or grocery store, but once you have the fat, you can reuse it. It also requires marinating overnight.

Makes 6 to 8 servings.

¼ cup kosher salt

1 tablespoon freshly ground black pepper

8 fresh thyme sprigs, leaves stripped off for use

3 bay leaves

2 teaspoons juniper berries

6 whole duck legs

2.5 pounds duck fat (this will yield about 5 cups)

1. In a small bowl, combine the salt, pepper, thyme leaves, bay leaves, and juniper berries. Rinse the duck legs with cold water and pat dry with paper towels. Place in a large baking dish and spread the salt rub evenly on all sides. Cover and refrigerate overnight to cure the meat.

2. When ready to cook the legs, place the duck fat in the slow cooker and put the heat on High to melt the fat. Remove the duck legs from the refrigerator and, one at a time, take them out of the pan and rinse them under cold water. Pat them dry with paper towels. When the fat is melted, add the legs to the cooker. The fat should stay at a simmer, so you'll want to turn the heat down to Low. Cover and cook on Low for about 4 hours. When cooked, the meat will be very tender and fall away from the bones.

3. Remove the cooked legs immediately, eating them right away or allowing them to cool for later use.

4. Put the fat from the slow cooker into a glass bowl that can fit the legs back into it and that can be securely sealed. When the fat and legs have cooled, put the legs into the bowl and refrigerate. The duck confit is good this way in the fridge for about 6 months. When ready to use, just remove a leg and allow it to come to room temperature so the fat can melt before using or eating.

> **Once you taste how good this is, you'll be eager to serve your lovely confit to family and friends. You can serve it in many ways, from as is— the just-cooked legs themselves—to shredded over salads, over sautéed greens, or just for delicious snacking. You can use the fat for roasting winter vegetables or other meats.**

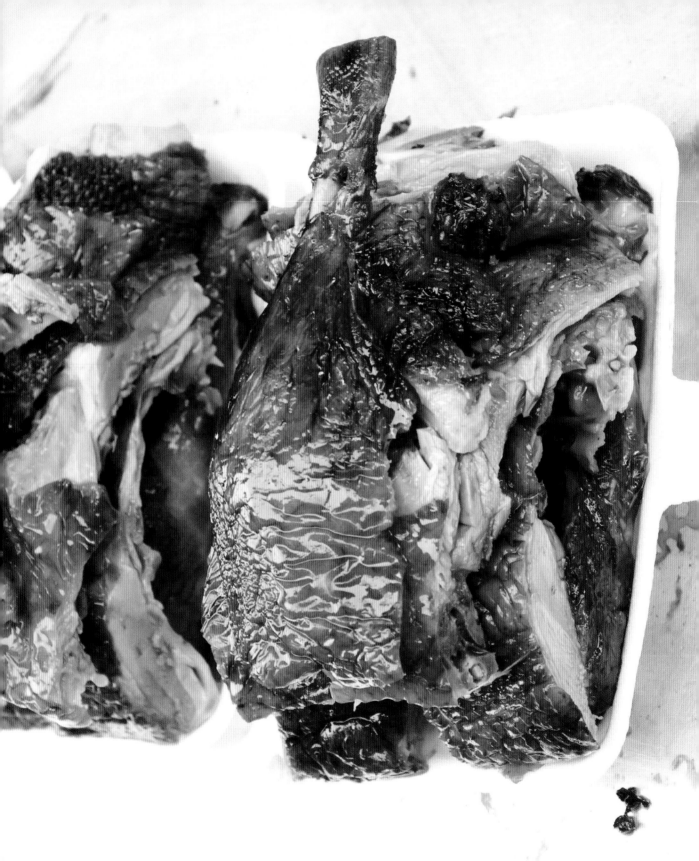

Soy and Ginger Duckling

Make this dish on a night when you know it's going to be really cold outside. The smells of the ginger, soy, and sherry used to season the duck will fill your kitchen while this is cooking and transport you to an exotic locale.

Makes 4 to 6 servings.

8 leeks

1 fresh duckling, 4 to 5 pounds

½ cup dry sherry

½ cup soy sauce

½ teaspoon sugar

½ teaspoon ginger

2 cloves garlic, minced

1¼ cup water

4 carrots, cut into strips

1. Prepare the leeks by cutting off the tough bottom, and also the top green parts, reserving only the white parts. Cut the leeks in half lengthwise, and rinse under cold water to remove any sand or dirt inside. When clean, cut the halves into half-moon slices about ¼-inch thick. Place in the bottom of the slow cooker.

2. Rinse the duck with cold water and remove any parts such as the neck and giblets. Pat the duckling dry and put it on top of the leeks in the slow cooker.

3. In a bowl, combine sherry, soy sauce, sugar, ginger and garlic, and stir to combine. Add the water, and pour the sauce over the duck. Cover and cook on Low for 6 to 8 hours or on High for 3 to 4 hours. In the last hour of cooking (whether on Low or High), turn the duck over and add the carrots. Finish cooking and serve.

For a dramatic, delicious, and more healthy side dish/presentation, serve the duck with the Festive Forbidden Rice recipe in Chapter 8.

Wild Goose a l'Orange

This is for everyone with friends or family who hunt game birds. The breasts of wild geese are lean and delicious if cooked properly. There is little to no fat, so it's important not to overcook the meat. If you don't have access to fresh game, you can purchase a goose in select grocery stores.

Makes 2 to 4 servings.

¼ cup bacon or duck fat (or olive oil)

2 whole breasts, halved, skin removed

½ teaspoon salt

¼ teaspoon pepper

2 small oranges, peeled, seeded, and segments halved

1 apple, cored and cubed

1 onion, cut into small wedges

6-oz can frozen orange juice concentrate, thawed

Heat fat in slow cooker on Low. Add goose breasts, flesh side down. Sprinkle with salt and pepper. Add orange segments, apple, onion, and orange concentrate. Cover and cook on Low for 6 to 8 hours, checking the meat to be sure it isn't overcooked, but that it is tender. When ready to serve, remove breasts, discarding fruit and onions. Season with additional salt and pepper.

While you won't be using the fruit sauce that the bird has cooked in as a gravy when serving, you can make a delicious ginger glaze for the meat. In a small saucepan, combine 1 tablespoon freshly grated ginger, 1 tablespoon fresh cilantro, chopped, 2 tablespoons honey, and about ½ cup water. Stir and bring to a boil, then remove from heat. Pour onto the meat or serve on the side.

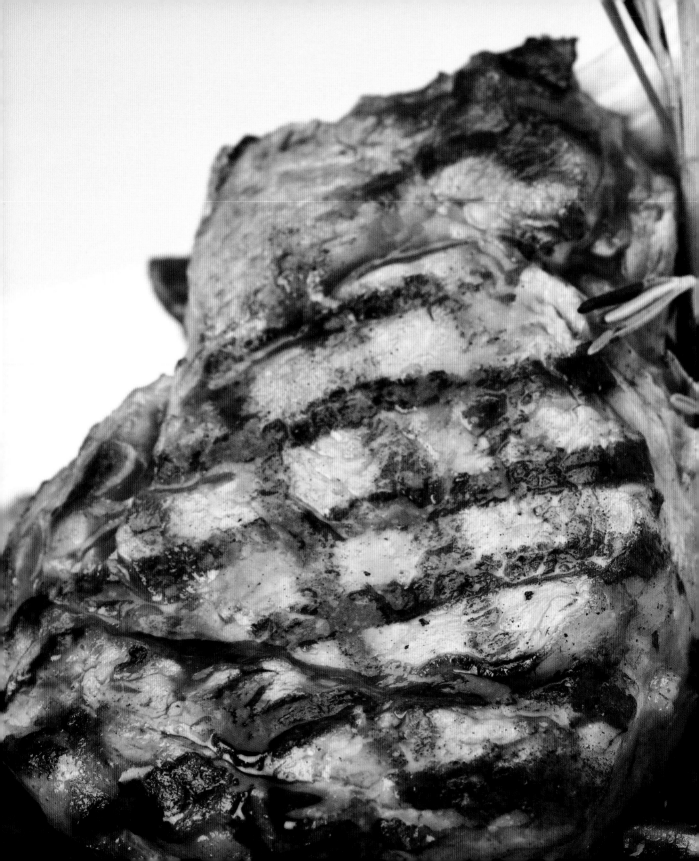

Veal Chops a la Magi

If the three kings were to descend on your house, you'd want to have this dish at the ready. It stars mushrooms and vermouth, which pair spectacularly with the delicate veal.

Makes 6 servings.

¼ cup flour
½ teaspoon salt
¼ teaspoon pepper
6 ½-inch thick-cut veal chops
4 tablespoons butter
2 cloves garlic, sliced thin
¼ pound sliced white mushrooms
¼ pound sliced Portobello mushrooms
⅔ cup dry Vermouth
Salt and pepper to taste
¼ cup chopped fresh parsley, for garnish

1. In a shallow soup bowl, combine the flour, salt and pepper. Dip each chop into the bowl to dust both sides of the chops. Set chops aside.

2. In a large skillet, heat 2 tablespoons butter over medium-high heat. Cook the chops in the butter 2 or 3 at a time to brown both sides, about 3 minutes a side. When browned, put the chops in the slow cooker. Add more butter if necessary to complete browning.

3. When meat is in the slow cooker, add the garlic, mushrooms, and Vermouth to the skillet. Lower the heat and stir to loosen the browned bits and just start the cooking of the mushrooms, about 5 minutes. Pour the mushrooms and sauce over the chops in the slow cooker.

4. Cover and cook on Low for 4 to 6 hours or on High for about 2 hours, or until chops are cooked through and tender. Serve with the mushrooms and sauce, and garnish with the chopped parsley.

> Vermouth is a fortified wine that can be made in sweet or dry variations. It's made with a proprietary blend of herbs and spices, and derives from the German word wermut, for wormwood, which was the earliest flavoring ingredient. Today, both sweet and dry vermouths are used in cocktails—and in cooking!

Chapter 7

Fish and Seafood Dishes

*W*hen I think of Christmas cooking and fish, I think of my husband's side of the family and their tradition of the seven fishes on Christmas Eve. While some of the fish could be—and was—served with pasta, the family wouldn't consider substituting a large lasagna or any other Italian extravagance for this special feast. There doesn't seem to be one easy answer as to how and why this tradition evolved, or which fishes should be eaten. It's ventured that this is a tradition of Southern Italy, where people are very superstitious. If it's a tradition, it's with good reason, and should be continued.

This chapter honors that tradition with seven fish recipes for the slow cooker—and one more for good measure. Maybe my sons will incorporate their grandparents' Christmas Eve fishes into a countdown of sorts so they can have fish but other things as well. Then they can make one of these recipes every day during the week leading up to Christmas Eve. I hope I will always find my place set at their table on this magical night.

Clam Sauce for Spaghetti

The recipe calls for canned clams, which are the heart of the sauce. But adding fresh clams or mussels will make it extra special and extra delicious.

Makes 4 servings.

Two 4-oz cans clams

8-oz bottle clam juice

2 tablespoons olive oil

1 garlic clove, minced

1 teaspoon fresh ginger, grated

½ teaspoon lemon zest

Salt to taste

1 pound littleneck clams or mussels, if desired, scrubbed clean

1. In a large bowl, combine clams, clam juice, olive oil, garlic, ginger, and zest. Stir well. Add salt to taste. Put in slow cooker, cover, and cook on Low for 4 to 5 hours or on High for 3 to 4 hours.

2. If desired, add the clams or mussels, put heat on low, cover, and cook an additional hour or so until shellfish opens.

3. Serve over bowls of thick spaghetti or linguine, and garnish with fresh parsley.

> It's now possible to find fresh minced clams in just about every supermarket. If they're not in the refrigerated case, check the freezer.

Tomato-Braised Tuna

Tuna is caught in the waters off Sicily, and in this recipe the gentle heat of the slow cooker glorifies this meaty fish while keeping it fairly rare. The herbs and tomatoes make a delicious sauce that you'll want to soak up with a piece of Italian bread.

Makes 4 to 6 servings.

1½- to 2-pound tuna fillet in one thick slice

¼ cup olive oil, divided

½ small red onion, chopped

3 cloves garlic, minced

15.5-oz can diced tomatoes

1 teaspoon fresh basil, chopped

¼ teaspoon dried oregano

½ teaspoon dried rosemary

3 tablespoons capers, drained and rinsed

2 tablespoons fresh parsley, chopped

1 bay leaf

Salt and pepper to taste

1. Soak tuna in cold water for 10 minutes. Pat dry with paper towels.

2. Heat 2 tablespoons of the oil in a large skillet over medium-high heat. Add onion and garlic and cook, stirring frequently, for 3 minutes, or until onion is translucent. Scrape mixture into the slow cooker. Add diced tomatoes, basil, oregano, rosemary, capers, parsley, and bay leaf to the slow cooker and stir well. Cook on Low for 2 to 3 hours or on High for about 1 hour.

3. Heat remaining oil in the skillet over medium-high heat. Add tuna, and brown well on both sides. Add tuna to the slow cooker, and cook on Low for an additional 2 hours or on High for an additional hour or 90 minutes. Tuna should be cooked but still rare in the center. Remove and discard bay leaf, season to taste with salt and pepper, and serve hot.

Soaking the tuna in water removes a lot of its remaining blood, so that the finished dish is lighter in color and not bright red. The same treatment can be used on other dark fish, such as mackerel or bluefish.

Hearty Shellfish Stew

This is the sort of fish stew that has become known as Cioppino in San Francisco and other American cities. It's made with red wine, in which you can thoroughly indulge for this incredible recipe.

Makes 4 to 6 servings.

¾ pound thick firm-fleshed fish fillets, such as cod, swordfish, or halibut

¾ pound sea scallops

¼ pound extra-large shrimp

A dozen mussels, scrubbed and debearded

3 tablespoons coconut oil

2 medium onions, diced

1 red bell pepper, seeds and ribs removed, and finely chopped

2 celery ribs, diced

3 cloves garlic, minced

2 tablespoons fresh oregano, chopped

2 teaspoon fresh thyme

28-oz can diced tomatoes, undrained

1½ cups dry red wine

1 cup fish stock

2 tablespoons tomato paste

1 bay leaf

¼ cup fresh parsley, chopped

3 tablespoons fresh basil, chopped

Salt and pepper to taste

1. Rinse fish and pat dry with paper towels. Remove and discard any skin of bones. Cut fish into 1-inch cubes.

2. Cut scallops in half. Peel and devein the shrimp. Refrigerate all seafood until ready to use, tightly covered with plastic wrap.

3. Heat oil in a medium skillet over medium-high heat. Add onions, red bell pepper, celery, garlic, oregano, and thyme. Cook stirring frequently, for 3 minutes, or until onions are translucent. Scrape mixture into the slow cooker.

4. Add tomatoes, wine, stock, tomato paste, and bay leaf to the slow cooker and stir well to dissolve tomato paste. Cook on Low for 5 to 7 hours or on High for 2 to 3 hours, until vegetables are almost tender.

5. If cooking on Low, raise the heat to High. Add seafood, parsley, and basil. Cook for 30 to 45 minutes, or until fish is cooked through. Remove and discard bay leaf, and season to taste with salt and pepper.

Variation:
Substitute squid for the sea scallops. Clean them, slice the bodies into ½-inch rings, and keep the tentacles whole.

Just-Done Salmon

The slight rare finish of this dish leaves the fish succulent and tasty. Once prepared, you can serve it with a number of different kinds of sauces, from a traditional tartar sauce to a fresh fruit salsa or just good old lemon!

Makes 4 to 6 servings.

4 salmon steaks (about 6 oz each), about ¾-inch thick

3 tablespoons olive oil

3 cloves garlic, minced

½ cup soy sauce

Salt and pepper to taste

1. Take a large piece of heavy duty aluminum foil and put the steaks in the middle. Position the fish on the foil in the slow cooker, positioning the sides of the foil so they come up and form a pocket around the fish.

2. In a small bowl, combine the oil, garlic, and soy sauce. Pour over the fish.

3. Secure the aluminum foil so the liquid won't come out. You should create a sealed pouch in which to cook the fish.

4. Cover the slow cooker and cook on Low for about 4 hours or on High for about 2 hours. The fish should be tender and flaky but still slightly pink inside. To serve, remove the foil and transfer the steaks to a plate.

Many of the thick, firm-fleshed fish like salmon, halibut, cod, tilapia, and flounder, can be purchased frozen. It's handy to keep a supply of fish fillets in your freezer. Dethawing them so they don't lose flavor or texture is the secret to successful recipes. We've found the best way is to put individual fillets in plastic baggies with air-tight seals, and then submerse in a bowl of cool (not warm!) water. It only takes about 15 minutes to thaw. Or put the frozen fillets in the refrigerator for several hours.

Brook Trout *Italiano*

The combination of garlic, oregano, basil, parsley, and rosemary make for a fragrant, delicious, and nutritious topping to this tender fish. The Broccoli Rabe recipe found in Chapter 9 makes a great side vegetable.

Makes 4 servings.

3 to 4 pounds brook trout fillets

¼ cup olive oil

2 cloves garlic, minced

1 teaspoon fresh oregano, chopped, or ¼ teaspoon dried

1 teaspoon fresh basil, chopped, or ½ teaspoon dried

1 teaspoon fresh parsley, chopped, or ½ teaspoon dried

1 teaspoon fresh rosemary, chopped, or ½ teaspoon dried

Juice of 1 lemon

¼ cup dry white wine

1. Place the fillets in the slow cooker. Add the garlic to the olive oil, and drizzle over the fish.

2. In a small bowl, combine the herbs and mix with a fork to blend without overly crushing. Sprinkle the herb mixture over the fish. Squeeze the lemon over the fish and add the wine.

3. Cook on Low for about 2 hours or on High for about 1 hour. The herbs will have made a thin carpet over the fish. Pour the juices from the cooker over the fish when serving. Season with salt and pepper.

It's easy to make your own Italian seasonings blend to have handy for seasoning fish, poultry, sauces, and even sprinkling on salads. Using dried herbs, combine 1 tablespoon each of the oregano, basil, parsley, and rosemary. Substitute 2 teaspoons garlic powder for the fresh garlic. Store in a small glass jar with an airtight lid.

Classic Calamari

No, they aren't fried—and your guests will be glad. When prepared in the slow cooker, calamari can be incredibly succulent and tender. Even skeptics will leave the table happy.

Makes 4 to 6 servings.

1 to 2 pounds squid, tubes and tentacles
1 tablespoon olive oil
1 onion, chopped
2 cloves garlic, crushed
1 cup fish stock or broth
1 lemon
1 teaspoon sugar
½ teaspoon salt
¼ teaspoon pepper

1. Rinse the tubes and tentacles with cold water and drain well. Slice the tubes into ¼-inch bands.

2. In a small skillet over medium-high heat, cook the onion in the oil until translucent, about 3 minutes. Add the garlic and stir. Transfer the mix to the slow cooker.

3. Put the squid in the slow cooker. Top with the fish stock and squeeze the juice from the lemon, being careful to remove the seeds. Add the sugar, salt, and pepper. Stir to combine all ingredients.

4. Cover and cook on Low for 3 to 4 hours. Test one of the pieces. It should be tender but cooked through. Don't let it go too long, as overcooked squid can get rubbery. If it's just about done and you are not ready to serve it, turn the slow cooker to Warm. It can stay at this setting for about another 30 minutes. Season with additional salt and pepper if desired.

Squid has long been on the dinner plates of Europeans, but it is only fairly recently that its popularity has risen here in the United States. When this member of the mollusk family began appearing on menus as fried calamari in the 1980s, it was an instant hit. Now it is a featured appetizer at most Italian restaurants—and many others. That's a good thing for us, as it's a delicious seafood whether fried, grilled, or slow-cooked.

Stuffed Calamari

This is a delicious and celebratory main course that pairs perfectly with a big green salad. The tubes cook up tender and juicy. If you have a large slow cooker, you can double the recipe.

Makes 4 servings.

2 pounds squid tubes, cleaned

½ cup golden raisins

¼ cup brandy

½ onion, chopped

2 tablespoons butter

1½ cups cooked rice

2 cups unseasoned breadcrumbs

1½ cups dry white wine

¼ teaspoon cayenne pepper

½ teaspoon lemon zest

¼ cup olive oil

¼ cup chopped fresh parsley

8.5-oz can diced tomatoes, with juice

Salt and pepper to taste

1. Make sure the squid bodies are thoroughly cleaned, and rinse them with cold water. Set aside.

2. In a small bowl, mix the raisins with the brandy. Let this combo sit while you prepare the rest of the stuffing.

3. In a skillet over medium-high heat, cook the onion in the butter until translucent, about 5 minutes. Add the rice and stir to combine, removing from heat.

4. In another bowl, pour the wine over the breadcrumbs and stir to combine. Add the onion-rice mixture, then the cayenne and lemon zest. Finally, add the soaked raisins and brandy. Stir the stuffing well.

5. Gently fill the squid tubes with the stuffing. Secure the open ends with a toothpick. Gently place stuffed calamari in the slow cooker. Drizzle with the olive oil, sprinkle the parsley over them, and top with the diced tomatoes.

6. Cover and cook on Low for 6 to 8 hours or on High for 2 to 3 hours, reducing heat to Low for another hour or two. The squid should be very tender. A longer, slower cooking is best.

Besides being low in fat and high in protein, calamari is also loaded with vitamins and minerals, including potassium, choline, phosphorous, calcium, magnesium, folate, iron, and vitamins A and C.

Sassy Shrimp

Give shrimp cocktail a run for its money during the holidays with this super-easy and super-tasty slow-cooked shrimp dish. Purchase uncooked shrimp for this recipe, and leave the tails on to make them easier to eat.

Makes 6 to 8 servings.

½ cup olive oil

4 cloves garlic, crushed

½ cup Asian chili sauce with soya bean oil, medium hot

2 tablespoons unsweetened coconut milk

2 pounds large raw shrimp (about 30), peeled up to the tails and deveined

1. In a bowl, combine the olive oil, garlic, chili sauce, and coconut milk. Whisk to combine. Pour into the slow cooker. Cover and cook on High for 20 to 30 minutes while you clean the shrimp.

2. Add cleaned shrimp to the hot sauce, and stir to coat the shrimp thoroughly. Cover and continue to cook on High for another 10 to 15 minutes until shrimp are cooked but not overdone.

3. Transfer the shrimp to a bowl or a serving dish with a slotted spoon. Pour the sauce into a bowl for dipping.

> Make sure you have plates and napkins a-plenty next to this dish when you serve it, as the sauce is runny and will certainly stain. But it's too tasty not to gobble up when it comes hot out of the slow cooker.

Chapter 8

Festive Sides

his chapter is dedicated to dishes featuring potatoes, rice, and pasta. They range from things as easy to get going as baked potatoes to dishes that showcase slow-simmering sauces rich with meats, peppers, and other spices. When the holiday table is laden with roast meats, these dishes shine. Or when you are invited to a potluck dinner, they're easy to prepare and take along.

So-Simple Risotto

Once you've made this Italian rice known for its porridge-like consistency in the slow cooker—without all the stirring of traditionally made risotto—you'll never do the stovetop version again!

Makes 4 servings.

3 tablespoons unsalted butter

1 medium white onion, chopped

1 cup Arborio rice

3 cups chicken broth

½ cup parmesan cheese

2 tablespoons fresh parsley, minced

Salt to taste

1. Heat butter in a medium saucepan over medium-high heat. Add onion and cook, stirring frequently, for 3 minutes or until onion is translucent.

2. Add rice and stir to coat grains. Raise the heat to high and add about ¼ to ½ cup broth. Stir for about two minutes, or until it is almost evaporated. Scrape mixture into the slow cooker.

3. Add the remaining broth to the slow cooker and stir well. Cook on high for 2 hours or until rice is soft and liquid is absorbed.

4. Stir in cheese and parsley, season with salt, and serve hot.

Risotto is one of Milan's contributions to Italian cuisine, and legend has it that it originated in the sixteenth century. True *risotto alla Milanese* is made with saffron, which perfumes the rice and creates a pale yellow dish. Today, almost any creamy rice dish with cheese added is called a risotto, but the authentic dish is made with Arborio rice, which, when cooked, releases a starch and creates its own sauce. The traditional dish requires constant stirring—a step happily unnecessary with the slow cooker version.

Melt in Your Mouth Mushroom Risotto

If you love mushrooms, you will love this dish—and you'll come to crave it for its total satisfaction!

Makes 4 servings.

3 tablespoons unsalted butter

1 medium onion, chopped

1 cup Arborio rice

2½ cups chicken broth

1 cup domestic mushrooms, trimmed and sliced

1 cup Portobello mushrooms, cut into 1-inch cubes

½ cup Parmesan cheese

Sprig of thyme for garnish

Salt to taste

1. Heat butter in a medium saucepan over medium-high heat. Add onion and cook, stirring frequently, for 3 minutes or until onion is translucent.

2. Add rice and stir to coat grains. Raise the heat to high and add about ¼ to ½ cup broth. Stir for about two minutes, or until it is almost evaporated. Scrape mixture into the slow cooker.

3. In the skillet, add both types of mushrooms and sauté in the oil that sticks to the pan for about 2 minutes or until the mushrooms are just soft, stirring constantly. Add the mushrooms to the slow cooker, then the remaining broth, and stir well. Cook on High for 2 to 3 hours or until rice is soft and liquid is absorbed. Stir in cheese, season with salt, and serve hot. Garnish with sprig of thyme.

Arborio rice is uniquely Italian and is named after the town in which it was developed. It is a short, fat grain with a pearly white exterior and high starch content, the result of less milling. Another of its characteristics is its ability to absorb flavors.

Scalloped Potatoes

Once you have the potatoes peeled and sliced, it's just a matter of stacking them in the slow cooker, adding the other ingredients, and returning to a masterpiece.

Makes 4 to 6 servings.

6 medium Idaho potatoes, thinly sliced

1 onion, thinly sliced

1 cup shredded cheddar cheese

½ cup fresh parsley, minced

½ cup milk

½ cup butter, melted

½ teaspoon paprika

Salt to taste

Non-stick cooking spray

1. Spray the inside of the slow cooker liberally with non-stick cooking spray.

2. In the slow cooker, alternate layers of potatoes, onions, cheese, and parsley until all are used up.

3. In a small bowl, combine the milk, butter, paprika, and salt. Pour this mixture over the ingredients in the slow cooker.

4. Cover and cook on Low for 7 to 9 hours or on High for 3 to 4 hours until potatoes are cooked through and bubbly. Serve hot.

This dish is classically prepared with heavy cream and lots of butter. While this makes an especially creamy dish, scalloped potatoes can be just as satisfying with far less fat and calories, as this recipe proves. The slow cooking renders the thinly sliced potatoes tender and tasty.

Indian Rice

The fragrant cumin and turmeric in this dish will awaken all your senses. It's delicious with almost any chicken dish.

Makes 6 servings.

4 cups brown rice

½ teaspoon ground cumin

½ teaspoon turmeric

3 tablespoons butter, cut into small pieces

4 cups chicken broth

4 cups water

Non-stick cooking spray

1. Spray the inside of the slow cooker liberally with non-stick cooking spray.

2. Add the rice to the slow cooker. Add spices and stir to combine.

3. Put the pieces of butter over the rice, then add the broth and water. Cover and cook on Low for 4 to 6 hours or on High for 2 to 3 hours. To keep rice from drying out too much or burning, check it about an hour before it should be ready, and if it's looking good, turn the cooker to warm. It can cook through on warm for several hours.

Brown rice is simply rice that has not been polished to remove the bran layer, as is done to produce white rice. Because only the hull is removed and the bran layer and germ are retained, brown rice has a nuttier flavor and chewier texture than white rice. It also has more vitamins, minerals, and fiber, as those are concentrated in the bran layer.

Herbed Polenta

Polenta hails from Italy, though it wasn't developed until corn started coming in from the New World. It's a corn "oatmeal" of sorts, and in this country it's most often cooked up for breakfast in place of grits, though it's developing more and more of a following in culinary circles.

Makes 4 servings.

5 cups chicken broth

1 cup fat milk

1 cup polenta (yellow corn meal)

½ teaspoon fresh parsley, chopped

½ teaspoon fresh thyme, chopped

½ teaspoon fresh rosemary, chopped

3 tablespoons unsalted butter

1 cup grated cheddar cheese

Salt to taste

Non-stick cooking spray

1. Spray the inside of the slow cooker liberally with non-stick cooking spray.

2. Combine the broth, milk, and polenta in the slow cooker. Whisk together thoroughly, cover, and cook on High for about 1½ hours, or until mixture begins to boil.

3. Open the slow cooker and add the herbs. Whisk again, cover and cook on High an additional 1½ hours, then turn heat to Low and cook for 2 or 3 more hours, or until polenta is very thick.

4. Stir in the butter and cheese, and season with salt. Serve hot.

An alternative way to serve polenta is to pack the hot polenta into a well-oiled loaf pan and chill it well. Once chilled you can cut it into slices and either grill or sauté them in butter or olive oil. You can also spread the polenta in a shallow baking dish to the thickness of ¾ inch, and then chill the mixture, cut it into long, narrow rectangles, and pan-fry them.

Mmmm Mashed Potatoes

Always welcome on the table, but especially so in the cold, dark months, mashed potatoes have a way of hitting the spot. They can even serve as a main course when paired with a couple of vegetable sides. Making them in the slow cooker is wonderfully easy.

Makes 8 to 10 servings.

10 large Golden potatoes, peeled and cubed

7 cups chicken stock or broth

1 cup light cream, warmed

1 cup (8 tablespoons) butter, cut into pieces

1 teaspoon salt (and more to taste)

½ teaspoon pepper (and more to taste)

1. Put the peeled and cubed potatoes and chicken stock in the slow cooker. Cover and cook on Low for about 6 hours or on High for about 4 hours, or until potatoes are tender.

2. With the slow cooker on Warm, mash the potatoes with the cream and butter. Add salt and pepper and stir. Add additional chicken broth, if needed, for desired consistency. Season with additional salt and pepper to taste.

Leftover mashed potatoes are wonderful to add to soups to thicken them. You can also form leftover mashed potatoes into small "cakes" and fry them in butter. Garnishing with fresh chopped parsley is always a tasty treat.

Savory Sausage Stuffing

Even if you stuff your bird, it's great to have an extra dish of stuffing. Using the slow cooker to prepare it frees up that much more room in your oven. Plus, the stuffing stays moist.

Makes 8 to 10 servings.

1 pound Italian sausage, sweet, spicy or a combination

3 large apples, peeled and cored

1 large onion, diced

1 cup diced celery

6 cups bread crumbs or 10 cups dried bread cubes

1 teaspoon fresh thyme, chopped

1 teaspoon salt

½ teaspoon pepper

3 eggs

6 cups chicken stock or broth

1 cup butter, cut into pieces

¼ cup fresh parsley, chopped

Salt and pepper to taste

1. Cut sausages into bite-sized pieces or cut casings and remove meat so that it is loose. In a large skillet over medium-high heat, cook sausage until browned and cooked through. Transfer cooked meat to a large bowl with a slotted spoon. Pour off all but ¼ cup fat from skillet. Add the apples, onion, and celery, and cook, stirring, until onions are translucent, about 5 minutes. Add the onion mix to the bowl with the sausage.

2. Stir the bread crumbs or cubed bread into the bowl with the sausage and onion mix. Add thyme, salt, and pepper, stirring to combine. Put seasoned bread into the slow cooker.

3. In the bowl in which the bread mixture was prepared, whisk the eggs together lightly and add the chicken stock. Whisk briefly to combine. Pour over bread mixture. Dot with the butter pieces.

4. Cover and cook on Low for 6 to 8 hours or on High for 4 to 5 hours. Transfer to a bowl to serve, garnishing with the chopped parsley.

There are lots of variations to stuffing recipes. Popular additions include dried fruits such as raisins or cranberries; nuts like toasted pine nuts, chestnuts, or walnuts; oysters; or squash. A traditional preparation tends to please the most people and also makes a great addition to soup.

Baked Potatoes

These are another crowd favorite, and not only do they cook up nicely in the slow cooker, but they can be kept warm there, too, giving you some leeway in the timing of your meal.

Cooks 4 to 8 potatoes.

4 to 8 russet potatoes (quantity will vary depending on the size of the potatoes and your slow cooker)

Aluminum foil

1. Wash and dry the potatoes. Wrap each potato in foil. Place the potatoes in the slow cooker.

2. Cook on Low for about 8 hours until tender when pierced with a knife.

Classic accompaniments to baked potatoes include butter (of course!), salt and pepper (definitely!), sour cream, and chives. You could do a baked potato toppings bar, though, and make the potatoes a really fun part of a buffet. Additional toppings include crumbled bacon, cheddar cheese, blue cheese, sautéed onions, sautéed mushrooms, or steamed broccoli bits. You can even include caviar if you want to get really fancy.

Slow-Roasted Red Potatoes

With the long slow cooking, you'll be pleasantly pleased to discover that the potatoes will even get crispy around the edges. The garlic and rosemary are delicious additions, and pair exceptionally well with pork, lamb, or beef.

Makes 4 to 6 servings.

6 tablespoons olive oil

8 small red potatoes, skins on and scrubbed clean

4 cloves garlic, minced

1 tablespoon fresh rosemary, coarsely chopped

1 teaspoon salt

½ teaspoon pepper

1. Put the oil in the slow cooker, cover, and set to High.

2. Clean the potatoes, cut them in half, and prepare the garlic and rosemary while the oil heats, about 15 minutes.

3. Add the potatoes, garlic, rosemary, salt, and pepper to the slow cooker and stir well, getting everything mixed and the potatoes well covered with the oil and seasonings.

4. Reduce heat to Low and cook for 5 to 6 hours, or keep heat on High and cook for about 3 hours, or until potatoes are tender. The skins should be browned. Serve with additional salt and pepper to taste.

Use flavored oils to vary this recipe. Try using olive oils infused with roasted garlic, truffle, basil, or hot peppers (or a combination). You'll want to omit the rosemary with anything but the roasted garlic or hot pepper oils, and you could add ½ cup diced Portobello mushrooms if you choose the truffle oil.

Cheesy Potato Casserole

We grown-ups can get fancy with our mashed or baked potatoes, but if you're looking to please kids of all ages, you'll want to turn to this recipe. It'll have them scooping out seconds or thirds.

Makes 4 to 6 servings.

6 to 8 Golden potatoes
7 tablespoons butter
1 tablespoon flour
1 cup milk, warmed to room temperature
2 cups grated sharp cheddar
Optional: crumbled bacon

1. Peel and quarter the potatoes. Rinse them off and pat them dry. Put them in the slow cooker and dot with 6 tablespoons butter. Cover and cook on Low for about 4 hours, until tender.

2. To make the cheese sauce: Melting 1 tablespoon of butter in a skillet over low to medium heat. When melted, add the flour and stir. Have the milk handy while you're cooking the flour. After about a minute, start gradually adding the milk. Stir quickly to mix without causing clumps. As the milk is incorporated, raise the heat slightly and continue to add milk. The sauce will thicken. When the milk is added, turn the heat to Low and stir in the grated cheese, 1 cup at a time. Get the sauce to the thickness and cheeziness you want by adding more milk or cheese.

3. Pour the cheese sauce into the potatoes and stir to combine.

4. Serve with crumbled bacon, if desired, or even more cheese.

> Using cheddar makes this dish a sure-thing for kids. You can cater it to an older crowd by using a different kind of cheese. Consider blue cheese or Gruyere or a Munster cheese. The recipe is easily doubled, too.

Baked Ziti

Are there enough days in the week for a fabulous dish of baked ziti? Not on my calendar. This recipe is great because you don't have to cook the pasta ahead of time.

Makes 4 to 6 servings.

28-oz can crushed tomatoes (no seasoning)

15-oz can tomato sauce

½ teaspoon dried oregano

1 teaspoon dried basil

1 teaspoon salt

½ teaspoon pepper

1 teaspoon onion powder

2 cloves garlic, pressed

1 teaspoon red pepper flakes (if desired)

1 pound penne or ziti, uncooked
2 cups shredded mozzarella cheese or
1 cup shredded mozzarella and 1 cup pizza blend cheese

1. In a bowl, mix together the crushed tomatoes, tomato sauce, oregano, basil, salt, pepper, onion powder, crushed garlic, and red pepper flakes. Stir to combine thoroughly.

2. Pour about $^1/_3$ of the sauce into the slow cooker. Add ½ of the pasta on top. Add another $^1/_3$ tomato sauce. Next, sprinkle with about ½ cup cheese. Add the remaining pasta, then sauce, then the rest of the cheese.

3. Cover and cook on Low for 4 hours or on High for 2 hours until pasta is cooked through and sauce is bubbling.

If you are asked to bring baked ziti to a party, make it in the slow cooker because you can just transport the whole thing there, keeping it on warm at the party instead of worrying about reheating it. If it's going to be sitting out for a while, bring a pasta sauce to serve on the side in case it gets dry.

Festive Forbidden Rice

Forbidden rice is black-grained rice that was once considered so rare and special that only the Chinese emperors could eat it. It is a thick-grained rice that cooks like Arborio rice. It has a wonderful whole-grain flavor. The color and texture will add an exotic touch to your holiday table.

Makes 6 to 8 servings.

2 cups Forbidden rice

3½ cups water

½ teaspoon salt

2 tablespoons unsalted butter

1. Rub the butter on the inside of the slow cooker to grease it lightly.

2. Add the rice, water, and salt.

3. Cover and cook on Low for about 4 hours and on High for about 2 hours. Be careful not to overcook.

Variation:

Add some color to the rice with the addition of sautéed vegetables. Consider diced fresh red and/or green peppers, or red peppers and broccoli florets, or even corn.

What makes black rice prized today is that, like brown rice, black rice has its outer layer, which is full of antioxidant-rich bran. It also contains anthocyanins, the pigments found in blueberries, acai, and some grapes, and which have increased antioxidant benefits linked to numerous health benefits.

Jasmine Rice Delight

This rice dish is as full of delightful flavors as a Christmas tree surrounded by gifts. It's wonderful to serve with chicken or pork.

Makes 4 to 6 servings.

1 tablespoons sesame oil

1 small onion, diced

2 jalapeno peppers, seeds removed and chopped (wear gloves to do this)

1 teaspoon cayenne pepper

2 teaspoons cinnamon

¼ teaspoon black pepper

½ cup cauliflower florets

2 carrots, peeled and sliced into rounds

1 small zucchini, cubed

2 cups jasmine rice

4 cups water

½ teaspoon salt

2 tablespoons golden raisins

½ cup raw, shelled cashews

1. In a large skillet over medium-high heat, heat the sesame oil and add the onions and jalapenos, stirring to cook for about 3 minutes.

2. Add the cayenne, cinnamon, and pepper, and stir to coat the onions and peppers. Add the cauliflower, carrots, and zucchini and stir. Put the mixture into the slow cooker.

3. Add the rice, water, and salt, and stir to combine.

4. Cover and cook on Low for 4 to 6 hours or on High for about 2 hours until rice is tender and vegetables are cooked. Add the raisins and cashews and heat through before serving.

> Jasmine rice originated in Thailand and has grown in popularity around the world. It has a fragrant, nutty aroma, and is characteristically less sticky when cooked than other varieties of rice. While it's available in brown and white versions (brown has the hull), the white rice is most preferred.

Tortellini in Meat Sauce

Because tortellini is a pasta concoction that cooks up quickly, it's not suitable for an all-day slow cooker preparation. However, it is the perfect thing to add to a slow-cooking sauce, where it'll cook until just ready. Serve with lots of freshly grated parmesan cheese.

Makes 4 to 6 servings.

1 pound ground turkey

1 small onion, diced

3 cloves garlic, minced

28-oz can crushed tomatoes with basil

½ pound mushrooms, chopped

Salt and pepper to taste

9-oz package fresh tortellini, or frozen tortellini that have thawed in the refrigerator

2 cups shredded mozzarella

1. In a large skillet over medium heat, cook the ground turkey until it is just beginning to brown. Add the onions and garlic and raise the heat slightly. Cook, stirring, until the meat is browned. Drain the fat, and add the tomatoes and mushrooms. Stir and season with salt and pepper.

2. Put the sauce in the slow cooker. Cover and cook on Low for 7 to 8 hours or on High for 4 to 5 hours, until mushrooms are tender. Add the tortellini, and sprinkle with the mozzarella. Cover and cook on Low an additional 20 minutes, or until tortellini is tender. Serve with grated parmesan and chopped parsley if desired.

If you can find tri-colored tortellini, this will make for a more colorful presentation. You can also use mini raviolis instead of tortellini.

Gnocchi

If you have older Italians among your family or friends, they can tell you stories of their grandmothers spending the morning making fresh gnocchi. These are essentially little clouds of pasta, made from potatoes, and so light that when cooked they float to the surface. This recipe finds them slow-cooking in a peppery sauce, which is wonderfully complementary.

Makes 4 to 6 servings.

2 tablespoons olive oil

1 medium onion, diced

2 cloves garlic, pressed

2 red peppers, seeded, cored, and cubed

1 green pepper, seeded, cored, and cubed

1 orange pepper, seeded, cored, and cubed

14-oz can chopped tomatoes

½ teaspoon dried basil

Salt and pepper to taste

Crushed red peppers to taste,

Pinch of sugar

1 cup chicken stock or broth

1 pound fresh or frozen gnocchi

1 cup grated Parmesan cheese

1. In a large skillet over medium-high heat, cook the onions and garlic in the olive oil until onions are translucent, about 3 minutes. Add the red, green, and orange peppers and cook until just heated through, about 2 minutes. Transfer the pepper and onion mix to the slow cooker.

2. Add the tomatoes and basil, and season with salt, pepper, crushed red pepper, and sugar. Stir to combine. Add the chicken stock.

3. Cover and cook on Low for 6 to 8 hours or on High for 4 to 5 hours.

4. With about 30 minutes left of cooking time, cook gnocchi according to package directions. Transfer from boiling water with a slotted spoon into the pepper sauce in the slow cooker. Stir to combine. Add Parmesan cheese and serve.

While it is commonly understood that gnocchi means "dumpling" in Italian, the word is closer in origin to the Italian *nocchio* (a knot in wood) or *nocca* (knuckle). And while synonymous with Italy, it is actually thought to have originated in the Middle East and then popularized through Europe with the spread of the Roman Empire. The earliest recipes were based on semolina flour, with the use of potatoes a relatively new occurrence. There are variations of gnocchi around the world, but the potato gnocchi we Americans know best hails from the Abruzzo region of Italy.

Chapter 9

Vegetable Dishes

While vegetables wouldn't be at the top of the list when asked about favorite foods for the holidays, there's only so much overindulging you can do before your body craves them. And the truth is, you'll feel better about the goodies you let yourself get away with through the holidays if you try to follow the simple rule of covering two-thirds of your plate with vegetables and only one-third with grain and/or protein.

Here's where the slow cooker comes to the rescue again. By being able to almost simply "toss" vegetables of your choice into it with various seasonings, turn it on, and let it prepare a yummy and satisfying dish for you, you can free up your time to do other things—including baking! The vegetables that work best in the slow cooker are the ones that need the most cooking time in general: carrots, fennel, peppers, artichokes, Brussels sprouts, cabbage, and several varieties of squash, for example.

These veggies form the base for dishes that might also include greens such as spinach, which takes no time to cook. The recipes explain when to add certain things so it all comes out right. Another bonus of these recipes is that many of them include garlic. Slow cooking minimizes the strength of garlic while retaining its nutrients, and garlic definitely boosts the autoimmune system, which helps fight off colds, which are often brought on by the stress and pace of the holidays.

There's no excuse for forgetting or overlooking vegetables on a daily basis, even in the busiest time of year, the holidays. These recipes prove how simple it can be.

Artichokes with Lemon and Herbs

The slow cooker is the simplest way to prepare artichokes.

Makes 4 to 6 servings.

4 to 6 artichokes, depending on size
of vegetables and the slow cooker

1 lemon, quartered

3 cloves garlic, crushed

1 teaspoon fresh rosemary, minced

2 cups water

1. Wash and pat dry the artichokes. Trim the stem to about ¼ inch from bottom. Pull off the first couple of layers of leaves at the bottom, and snip the pointy ends off the leaves all around the chokes.

2. Place the artichokes in the slow cooker, bottoms down. Squeeze the juice of the lemons over the artichokes and put the squeezed quarters in with the artichokes, distributed throughout. Peel the garlic cloves and crush with the back of a knife. Put the garlic cloves in the slow cooker, distributed throughout. Sprinkle the rosemary around the artichokes.

3. Pour the water around the artichokes so that it covers the bottom of the slow cooker with about ½ to 1 inch of water. Cover and cook on Low for 6 to 8 hours or on High for 4 to 5 hours. Artichokes should be tender, with leaves easily breaking away from the core. Serve hot or at room temperature with the lemon/garlic juice as a dipping sauce for the leaves.

Artichokes are a lot of fun to eat as you work your way through the leaves to what is considered the vegetable's most delicious part, its heart. Peel each leaf off and dip the bottom into the lemon/garlic cooking liquid, or into some melted coconut butter. Put the leaf in your mouth, press down with your teeth, and scrape the tender flesh from the lower part of the leaves. Work through the artichoke until the leaves are small and nearly transparent. Pull off the last tip of leaves. The heart will be left, attached to the stem. There is some "fuzz" on the top of the heart that needs to be gently scraped off, as it can be bitter. It falls off easily. Now enjoy the heart!

Roasted Tomatoes

Because the slow cooker retains the moisture in foods, these won't need to cook long to become moist and flavorful. Seasoned with some herbs and garlic, they make a colorful and tasty side dish.

Makes 4 to 6 servings.

4 large, ripe tomatoes, cut in half, seeds removed

2 cloves garlic, minced

1 teaspoon fresh oregano, minced, or ½ teaspoon dried

Salt and pepper to taste

1 teaspoon fresh parsley, chopped

1. Place cut tomatoes bottom down in the slow cooker.

2. Sprinkle minced garlic on top, then sprinkle with oregano.

3. Cover and cook on Low for 3 to 4 hours or on High for 1 to 2 hours.

4. Season with salt and pepper, and garnish with parsley.

> **Slow cooking brings out the flavor in off-season tomatoes.**

Glazed Carrots

Adding a hint of something sweet to slow-cooked carrots turns them from tasty to terrific.

Makes 4 to 6 servings.

2 pounds carrots, peeled and cut quartered lengthwise into 4-inch sticks

½ cup vegetable broth or water

1 tablespoon coconut crystals or maple syrup

1 teaspoon olive oil

2 tablespoons fresh parsley or dill, chopped

1. Place carrot sticks in slow cooker. In a small bowl, combine the broth or water, coconut crystals or syrup, and olive oil. Pour the liquid over the carrots.

2. Cover and cook on Low for 2 to 3 hours until carrots are tender. Open the lid and keep it propped open with the handle of a wooden spoon, and continue to cook for 20 to 30 minutes until some liquid is cooked off and the carrots glaze.

3. Garnish with fresh parsley or dill before serving.

Carrots could be considered "candy"—a vegetable that also has a fairly high sugar content. Fortunately that sugar is naturally occurring and a "treat" in the truest sense of the word. Carrots are loaded with other vitamins and minerals, most notably beta carotene, from which they get their color. The brighter the better!

Italian-Style Peppers

This recipe is soooooooooo easy! You'll love it! Slice the peppers, toss them with some olive oil and garlic, put everything in the slow cooker, and return to a mountain of tender peppers that are the perfect accompaniment to any roasts or other simple meat or fish dishes.

Makes 8 to 10 servings.

6 to 8 bell peppers (use a combo of green, red, yellow, and orange for the most color and flavor)

4 tablespoons olive oil

1 teaspoon salt

½ teaspoon pepper

2 tablespoons balsamic vinegar

1. Prepare the peppers by cutting out the core and removing all seeds. Slice the peppers into ¼-inch wide long strips.

2. In a large bowl, combine olive oil, salt, pepper, and balsamic vinegar. Add the peppers and stir to coat thoroughly. Put the peppers into the slow cooker.

3. Cover and cook on Low for 5 to 7 hours or on High for 3 to 4 hours until tender and fragrant.

If you've ever wondered why red bell peppers are always more expensive than green, it's because they are the same peppers but they've been left on the plant to mature. That's why they're sweeter and less acidic than green peppers. But they are also more perishable to ship, which accounts for their premium price.

Brussels Sprouts with Bacon

Slow cooking this earthy veggie mellows its tanginess but brings out its woodsy depth of flavor. The smoky bacon, a touch of mustard, and seasoning with just a hint of sea salt add the perfect finish.

Makes 4 to 6 servings.

2 pounds Brussels sprouts

½ pound thick-cut bacon

3 tablespoons olive oil

1 teaspoon dry mustard

½ cup water

Pinch of sea salt

1. Wash and trim the Brussels sprouts, cutting off the coarsest part of the bottom and a layer or so of the leaves on the bottom. Cut the sprouts in half, and put them in the slow cooker.

2. In a large skillet, cook the slices of bacon over medium-high heat, turning to cook both sides until crisp. Drain on a plate covered with a paper towel and allow to cool.

3. In a measuring cup, mix the olive oil, dry mustard, and water. Pour over the Brussels sprouts. Sprinkle with crumbled bacon. Cover and cook on Low for 3 to 4 hours or on High for 2 to 3 hours. Before serving, add a pinch of sea salt.

While the mustard and bacon combine for a wonderful tanginess to this recipe, you can omit the bacon and substitute other spices to get different flavors. For spicier sprouts, add some cayenne pepper or Asian chili sauce; for an Indian taste, add hints of curry or cumin.

Sweet Potatoes and Apples

This is a New England version of candied sweet potatoes, with applesauce and maple syrup providing moisture while cinnamon adds a bit of aroma and spice. Serve it with any simple poultry or pork dish, and even with game meats such as venison.

Makes 4 to 6 servings.

1 tablespoon butter (for greasing the slow cooker)

3 large sweet potatoes or yams, peeled and thinly sliced

2 Granny Smith apples, peeled, cored, and thinly sliced

1 cup chunky applesauce

2 tablespoons maple syrup

2 tablespoons brown sugar

6 tablespoons unsalted butter, melted

¼ teaspoon ground cinnamon

Pinch of salt

1. Grease the inside of the slow cooker with butter.

2. Arrange half the sweet potatoes and apples in the slow cooker. Combine applesauce, maple syrup, brown sugar, melted butter, cinnamon, and salt in a mixing bowl. Pour half the mixture over the sweet potatoes and apples, and repeat with remaining potatoes, apples, and mixture.

3. Cook on Low for 6 to 8 hours or on High for 3 to 4 hours, or until sweet potatoes are tender.

Although sweet potatoes and yams are used interchangeably in recipes, they are different tubers. Yams are native to Africa and have a flesh that is lighter in color but sweeter than sweet potatoes. Yams also have a higher moisture content, so cut back slightly on liquids if you are using an authentic yam in a dish.

Roasted Beets

If you love beets, you'll love this method of cooking them. It "beats" waiting a long time for them to cook in boiling water! The color is wonderful this time of year, too (if you live in a northern climate).

Makes 6 to 8 servings.

2 bunches beets with tops (about 2 pounds)

2 tablespoons olive oil

1 clove garlic, minced

Greens from the beets, washed and cut into 1-inch pieces

Salt to taste

1. Scrub the beets clean and cut into 1-inch pieces.

2. Heat the oil in a medium skillet over medium-high heat and add the garlic. Cook, stirring constantly, about 1 minute. Add the beet greens and continue cooking and stirring until greens are just wilted, about 3 minutes.

3. Put beets into the slow cooker, topping with the greens. Cover and cook on Low for 4 to 5 hours, or on High for 3 to 4 hours, or until beets are soft.

4. Season with salt and serve.

Betacynin is the name of the pigment that gives red beets their deep color. Some people's bodies aren't able to process betacynin during digestion. As a result, their urine may be colored pink. This is temporary and is in no way harmful.

Broccoli Rabe

Consider this your "lazy" way to great broccoli rabe. The longer this slow cooks, the better, and if you put it on warm after 8 hours, it can go a few more hours. Or you can make it up to several days ahead and refrigerate until ready to reheat and serve. This is often served with the fish dishes in Chapter 7 as part of a traditional Italian Christmas Eve feast.

Makes 4 to 6 servings.

1 pound broccoli rabe

6 large cloves garlic, sliced

1 teaspoon red pepper flakes

⅓ cup extra virgin olive oil

Salt to taste

1. Prepare the broccoli rabe by removing the tough stems and setting aside only the tops and the tender parts of the stems. Put these in a colander and rinse, then spin and/or pat dry.

2. Put the prepared broccoli rabe in the slow cooker, and add the garlic, red pepper flakes, and olive oil. Cover and cook on Low for 6 to 8 hours (do not cook on High). Season with salt to taste.

> Broccoli rabe is related to broccoli, and is a member of the turnip family. It is definitely more bitter than broccoli, and has long been popular in Italy and Portugal.

Garlic Mashed Cauliflower

This super-simple recipe produces a flavorful and creamy dish. The roasted garlic produces so much flavor that you don't have to season the mashed vegetables with a lot of butter or salt, as you would with more traditional mashed potatoes.

Makes 6 to 8 servings.

Two 14-oz bags of frozen cauliflower florets
Hot water to cover
1 small head of garlic, roasted
1 tablespoon olive oil
¼ to ½ cup heavy cream
Salt and pepper to taste

1. Put the cauliflower in the slow cooker and add hot tap water until the florets are just covered. Cover and cook on Low for 4 to 5 hours or on High for 2 to 3 hours until cauliflower is tender. Drain the cauliflower and put it in a bowl.

2. Add the roasted garlic cloves and the oil, and mash with a potato masher or puree with an immersion blender, mashing to desired consistency. Stir in ¼ cup of the heavy cream, adding more if desired for taste and consistency. Season with salt and pepper.

While the cauliflower is cooking in the slow cooker, roast the garlic. To do this, preheat the oven to 400 degrees F. Peel off the outermost layers of skin on a whole clove of garlic, and cut off about ¼ to ½ inch from the top so the cloves are exposed. Put the head on a baking pan (like a muffin tin or cake pan), and drizzle about a teaspoon of olive oil on the top, being sure to coat it. Cover with aluminum foil and bake for about 30 to 40 minutes. Allow to cool before squeezing out cloves.

Freezer-Section Veggies

We snuck this one in because we know you want to keep your commitment to vegetables but you are time challenged! One of the joys of a slow cooker is that you can put something like this together quickly and trust it will come out tasting great.

Makes 4 to 6 servings.

Two 16-oz bags of frozen vegetables (mix and match broccoli, cauliflower, brussel sprouts, pearl onions, or a mix with water chestnuts)

2 tablespoons olive oil

1 small onion, diced

2 cloves garlic, minced

1 cup water or vegetable stock or broth

Salt and pepper to taste

1. Put frozen vegetables into the slow cooker.

2. In a small skillet over medium-high heat, add the olive oil, onions, and garlic and cook, stirring, until onions are translucent, about 3 minutes. Scrape mixture into slow cooker.

3. Add water or vegetable broth. Cover and cook on Low for 4 to 5 hours or on High for 2 to 3 hours until vegetables are tender. Season with salt and pepper to taste.

> Get creative with the seasonings you add to the veggies. You can sprinkle some cumin or curry powder in with the onions and garlic, or add a teaspoon of fresh-chopped rosemary. Fresh parsley and lemon are always great additions before serving.

Braised Fennel and Chard

Fennel has an almost silky texture and sweet flavor once it's braised. Swiss chard is a hearty green that adds a touch of color and lots of extra vitamins.

Makes 4 to 6 servings.

2 medium fennel bulbs

2 tablespoons butter

½ small onion, thinly sliced

1 clove garlic, minced

1 cup vegetable stock or broth

1 teaspoon fresh thyme, or
¼ teaspoon dried

1 pound Swiss chard, coarse stems removed, and ripped into large pieces

Salt and pepper to taste

1. Cut stalks off fennel bulb, trim root end, and cut bulb in half through the root. Trim out core, then slice fennel into 1-inch-thick slices across the bulb. Arrange slices in the slow cooker, and repeat with second bulb.

2. Heat butter in a small skillet over medium heat. Add onion and garlic and cook, stirring frequently, for 3 minutes, or until onion is translucent. Scrape mixture into the slow cooker.

3. Add stock and thyme to the slow cooker. Cook on Low for 3 to 4 hours or on High for about 2 hours, or until fennel is tender. Add the Swiss chard and continue to cook on Low for another 2 hours, or on High for another hour. Season to taste with salt and pepper.

> Although the celery-like stalks are trimmed off the fennel bulb for this dish, don't throw them out. They add a wonderful anise flavor as well as a crisp texture when used in place of celery in salads and other raw dishes.

Lean Green Beans

Fibrous and crunchy green beans turn into succulent and flavorful green beans when made in the slow cooker. It can be challenging at this time of year, but start with the freshest vegetables you can find.

Makes 6 to 8 servings.

2 pounds fresh green beans

8 to 10 cherry tomatoes, halved

2 tablespoons olive oil

1 small red onion, diced

½ teaspoon dried thyme

½ cup dry white wine

Salt and pepper to taste

1. Snip off the ends of the beans and remove the "string" that runs the length of the bean if it reveals itself. Rinse the beans under cold water, and put them in the slow cooker. Add the cherry tomatoes.

2. In a small skillet over medium-high heat, cook the onion in the oil until just translucent, about 2 minutes. Remove from the heat and stir in the thyme. Put over beans in the slow cooker.

3. Add the white wine. Cover and cook on Low for 2 to 3 hours. Season with salt and pepper.

No one else will notice, but this dish features red and green ingredients—ho, ho, ho!

Roasted Root Vegetables

If you like to shop farmers markets in the winter, you can often find a nice variety of root vegetables. Feel free to mix and match to your taste. Butternut squash is a great veggie to add to the mix, too.

Makes 4 to 6 servings.

1 large turnip, peeled and cubed

1 large parsnip, peeled and cubed

1 large potato, peeled and cubed

1 medium butternut squash, peeled, seeds removed, and cut into cubes

1 sweet onion, cut into thin wedges

6 cloves garlic, sliced thin

½ cup extra-virgin olive oil

Salt and pepper to taste

1. In a large bowl, combine the cubed turnip, parsnip, potato, and squash, the onion wedges, and the sliced garlic.

2. Put everything into the slow cooker. Cover with the olive oil, and sprinkle with salt and pepper.

3. Cover and cook on Low for 5 to 6 hours, or on High for 3 to 4 hours, until vegetables are soft and fragrant.

Variations:
Substitute a large sweet potato or 3 or 4 carrots for the butternut squash.

Chapter 10

Decadent – and Simple – Desserts

oliday desserts range from the grand and gluttonous to the simple and satisfying; from needing to be as special as the main course (if not more so), to versatile enough to take to a last-minute potluck.

The selection here is intended to serve this diversity, from some easy box cake-inspired creations to richer and denser sweets like the Banana Bomb or Amazing Almond cake. Serving whipped cream with the dessert is a frequent recommendation, as slow-cooker desserts aren't conducive to frosting. For an extra-special treat, you can flavor the whipped cream with a liqueur such as Kahlua, Amaretto, Frangelico, Grand Marnier, or Godiva Chocolate.

Chocolate Pudding Cake

Moist and flavorful, this is a recipe you'll be using when you know you have friends coming over, or a gathering of your kids' friends, or just because. We prefer the darkest chocolate available, but you can choose regular chocolate pudding mix or even milk chocolate chips.

Makes 6 to 8 servings.

1 package chocolate cake mix

1⅔ cup water

3 large eggs

⅓ cup canola oil

2 cups cold milk (2% is best)

1 package chocolate fudge instant pudding mix

12-oz bag dark chocolate chips

Non-stick cooking spray

1. Spray the inside of the slow cooker liberally with non-stick cooking spray.

2. In a large bowl, combine the cake mix, water, eggs and oil. Using an electric mixer, beat on low speed for 30 seconds, then increase the speed to medium and beat for another 2 minutes. Transfer this to the slow cooker.

3. In another bowl, use a whisk to combine milk and pudding mix, whisking for 2 minutes. Let stand until just set, about 2 minutes. Spoon the pudding mixture over the cake batter, then sprinkle with the chocolate chips.

4. Cover and cook on Low for 4 to 5 hours or on High for about 3 hours. Test for doneness by inserting a toothpick in the center. It should come out with moist crumbs. Don't overcook. Serve warm out of the slow cooker.

If you want to serve this cake on a platter, instead of spraying the slow cooker with the non-stick spray, line it with tin foil, being sure to bring the sides up and over the top. When the cake is done, lift out the foil and invert the cake onto a platter. It can be iced with a frosting when cool, or spread with whipped cream and/or fresh fruit.

Luscious Lemon Cake

A lemony sweet is a wonderful change of pace from the preponderance of chocolate served up during the holidays. This fragrant cake is sunshine in your spoon.

Makes 6 to 8 servings.

1 package lemon cake mix

1⅓ cup water

⅓ cup fresh-squeezed lemon juice

Zest from 1 lemon

3 large eggs

⅓ cup canola oil

2 cups cold milk (2% is best)

1 package lemon instant pudding mix

Non-stick cooking spray

1. Spray the inside of the slow cooker liberally with non-stick cooking spray.

2. In a large bowl, combine the cake mix, water, lemon juice, zest, eggs, and oil. Using an electric mixer, beat on low speed for 30 seconds, then increase the speed to medium and beat for another 2 minutes. Transfer this to the slow cooker.

3. In another bowl, use a whisk to combine milk and pudding mix, whisking for 2 minutes. Let stand until just set, about 2 minutes. Spoon the pudding mixture over the cake batter.

4. Cover and cook on Low for about 3 hours or on High for about 2 hours. Test for doneness by inserting a toothpick in the center. It should come out with moist crumbs. Don't overcook. Serve warm out of the slow cooker.

Serve this cake with a lemon glaze to really take the taste over the top. Make it by combining 2 tablespoons fresh-squeezed lemon juice with 1 cup confectioner's sugar, stirring well to mix thoroughly. Spoon over cake while warm.

Very Berry Sauce

This sauce is a liqueur-infused berry topping. This sauce is a winner on these and other desserts: brownies, chocolate cake, ice cream, pound cake, cheesecake, angel food cake, granola, and of course, fresh fruit. Or make extra and give it as gifts.

Makes about 2 cups.

1 pound fresh strawberries, tops removed

6-oz package fresh blueberries

6-oz package fresh raspberries

½ cup sugar

¼ cup orange-flavored liqueur

Grated peel and juice of 1 medium orange (seeds removed)

Non-stick cooking spray

1. Spray 3½- to 4-quart slow cooker with non-stick cooking spray.

2. In a large bowl, combine the fruits, sugar, liqueur, grated peel, and orange juice. Stir thoroughly.

3. Transfer to slow cooker, cover, and cook on Low for 5 to 6 hours or on High for 2 to 3 hours until thickened. Check the consistency with about 1 hour of cooking time left to be sure you don't overcook it.

If it's difficult for you to find fresh berries, you can substitute frozen fruit. Be sure to thaw it first, and discard about ½ the juice.

Rice Pudding

Once you master this simple recipe, you can add fruits and flavorings to it. Its creamy goodness makes it taste like it's more calories than it is.

Makes 4 servings.

1 cup Arborio rice

14-oz can unsweetened coconut water

14-oz can condensed milk

2 cups milk

½ teaspoon cinnamon or nutmeg

Pinch of salt

Raspberries (for topping)

Non-stick cooking spray

1. Spray the inside of the slow cooker liberally with non-stick cooking spray.

2. Combine rice, coconut water, condensed milk, milk, cinnamon or nutmeg, and salt in the slow cooker. Stir well.

3. Cook on Low for 5 to 7 hours, or on High for 2 to 3 hours. Rice should be soft and the liquid thick when it is thoroughly cooked.

4. Serve hot, warm, or chilled, and top with raspberries.

Raspberry-Pear Cobbler

Serve this along with the recipe for barbeque ribs to make a summer-themed menu for a non-traditional holiday dinner.

Makes 4 servings.

1 cup all-purpose flour

¾ cup brown sugar

1 teaspoon baking powder

¼ teaspoon salt

¼ teaspoon ground cinnamon

¼ teaspoon ground nutmeg

2 eggs, lightly beaten

3 tablespoons vegetable oil

2 tablespoons milk

4 cups fresh or frozen raspberries

2 cups fresh or frozen Bosc pears, cored and cut into cubes

1 cup water

3 tablespoons quick-cooking tapioca

½ cup maple syrup

1. In a medium bowl, stir together flour, 3/4 cup brown sugar, baking powder, salt, cinnamon, and nutmeg. In a small bowl, combine eggs, oil, and milk. Add egg mixture all at once to flour mixture. Stir just until moistened. Set aside.

2. In a large saucepan, combine berries and pears, the water, and tapioca. Bring to a boil. Add maple syrup to hot fruit mixture, remove from heat, and put into the slow cooker. Immediately spoon the batter over the fruit mixture.

3. Cover and cook on Low for 4 to 5 hours or on High for 1 to 2 hours. Test for doneness by inserting a toothpick in the center. If it comes out clean, it's done. When done, turn the cooker off, leave uncovered, and let stand for about 30 minutes hour to cool. Serve warm.

You can use frozen berries if you can't get your hands on fresh ones in the middle of winter.

Indian Pudding

This thick and rich pudding is a wonderful fall or winter dessert, rich with maple syrup and brown sugar.

Makes 4 servings.

5 cups milk
¼ cup firmly packed brown sugar
½ cup maple syrup
¾ cup yellow cornmeal
6 tablespoons unsalted butter
¼ teaspoon vanilla extract
1 teaspoon fresh ginger, grated
Pinch of salt
Non-stick cooking spray

1. Combine milk, brown sugar, and maple syrup in a 2-quart saucepan, and stir well. Heat over medium heat, stirring occasionally, until mixture comes to a boil. Whisk in cornmeal and simmer mixture, whisking frequently, for about 10 minutes or until thick.

2. Stir butter and vanilla into the mix, and whisk until butter melts. Remove the pan from the heat. Stir in the ginger and pinch of salt.

3. Spray the inside of the slow cooker with non-stick cooking spray. Using a spatula, transfer all of the pudding mixture into the slow cooker. Cover and cook on Low for 3 to 5 hours (do not cook on High).

4. When the edges have darkened slightly and the center is set, the pudding is done. Turn off the cooker, uncover, and let cool until warm before serving.

Banana Bomb Cake

The banana-rum flavor combination in this cake is outstanding. It's a great way to turn those very ripe bananas into something extraordinary.

Makes 4 to 6 servings.

2 tablespoons butter, softened, for greasing the aluminum foil

¾ cup firmly packed brown sugar

1 tablespoon rum (dark rum is best)

1 tablespoon water

6 medium-sized, ripe bananas, peeled and sliced into circles

¾ cup flour

¾ teaspoon baking powder

½ teaspoon cinnamon

¼ teaspoon nutmeg

¼ teaspoon salt

4 tablespoons butter

1¼ cups sugar

1 whole egg, and 1 egg separated (yolk only)

2 tablespoons low-fat milk

Non-stick cooking spray

Aluminum foil

Vanilla ice cream to serve with the cake

1. Liberally spray the inside of the slow cooker with non-stick cooking spray. Line the entire slow cooker with aluminum foil (sides can extend over the top). Grease the aluminum foil with a tablespoon or two of the butter, softened, so it is covered thoroughly.

2. Sprinkle brown sugar over the bottom of the slow cooker. Drizzle the rum and water over the sugar. Position the bananas over the sugar, pressing them in securely but without squishing them. Turn the cooker to High and leave uncovered while you prepare the cake.

3. In a large bowl, combine flour, baking powder, salt, cinnamon, and nutmeg. Use a whisk to combine the ingredients thoroughly.

4. In a medium-sized bowl, use an electric mixer to beat the butter and sugar until just blended, then beat on high speed until the mixture is light and fluffy. Add the whole egg and beat on a lower speed until combined. Add the egg yolk and beat until combined.

5. With the beaters on low or medium, begin adding the flour mixture. Working in batches, beat in about $1/3$ of the flour, then 1 tablespoon milk, more flour, milk, and ending with the flour.

6. When the batter is smooth, pour it over the bananas and sugar in the slow cooker. Using a double layer of paper towels, cover the top of the cooker before fitting it with the actual cover. This will create a tighter seal and help absorb excess liquid.

7. Cover securely and let cook on High for 3 to 4 hours, or until edges are slightly browned and the cake is springy to the touch. Turn off the cooker and let rest for about 15 minutes.

8. Lift the cake from the slow cooker using the aluminum foil. Allow to cool out of the cooker for about half an hour, then invert onto a plate before serving so bananas are showing.

9. Serve with a scoop of vanilla ice cream while the cake is still warm.

Chocolate Fondue

Here is a treat that you can prepare in the slow cooker for short-notice occasions. It only needs about an hour of cooking time. While this is happening (and you don't need to stir), you can cut up things to dip into it, like bananas, apples, pound cake, pretzels, and other goodies.

Makes 4 servings.

¾ pound good-quality bittersweet chocolate, chopped

½ cup heavy whipping cream

3 tablespoons liqueur or liquor or rum extract if you want a non-alcoholic fondue

1. Combine chocolate, cream, and liqueur or extract in the slow cooker. Cook on Low for 45 to 60 minutes, or until chocolate melts. Stir gently toward the end of the cooking time.

2. Serve directly from the slow cooker, using large toothpicks or fondue forks to dip the selection of foods.

> The fondue can be flavored with any number of liqueurs or liquors, including rum, bourbon, tequila, brandy, triple sec, kirsch, crème de cacao, Irish Cream, raspberry liqueur, or even chocolate liqueur.

Full of Fall Cake

This moist cake is a great treat any time of year, but during the holidays the cinnamon makes it seem especially festive.

Makes 6 servings.

3 cups unsweetened chunky apple sauce

2 cups flour

1 cup brown sugar

¼ cup maple syrup

1 cup canned pumpkin

3 eggs, beaten

⅓ cup vegetable oil

2 teaspoons baking powder

¼ teaspoon baking soda

Pinch salt

1 teaspoon cinnamon

¼ teaspoon nutmeg

2 cups buttercream frosting

Non-stick cooking spray

1. Liberally spray the slow cooker with non-stick cooking spray. Put applesauce in the bottom and spread evenly to cover.

2. In a large bowl, combine flour, brown sugar, syrup, pumpkin, eggs, vegetable oil, baking powder, baking soda, salt, cinnamon, and nutmeg. Beat with electric mixer on medium until combined, and then for another 2 minutes, scraping the sides of the bowl. Use a spatula to transfer the cake mixture to the slow cooker and over the applesauce mixture.

3. Double layer some paper towels and place over the top of the cooker to absorb any additional moisture. Cover the slow cooker as usual, and cook on High for 2 hours or until a toothpick inserted in the center comes out clean. When cool, frost with buttercream frosting.

Panettone Bread Pudding

Panettone is a sweet yeast bread that originated in Milan and is traditionally served at Christmas. It usually contains some sort of dried fruit as well as candied citrus peel.

Makes 6 to 8 servings.

3 large eggs

1 cup sugar

1¾ cup whole milk

6 tablespoons unsalted butter, melted

½ teaspoon pure vanilla extract

¼ teaspoon ground cinnamon

Pinch of salt

5 cups cubed Panettone

¼ cup golden raisins

½ cup mixed candied fruits

Non-stick cooking spray

Whipped cream (optional)

1. Whisk eggs in a large mixing bowl with sugar until thick and lemon-colored. Whisk in milk, melted butter, vanilla, cinnamon, and salt. Add bread cubes, and press down with the back of a spoon so they absorb the egg mixture. Stir in raisins and candied fruit.

2. Spray the slow cooker liberally with non-stick cooking spray. Spoon the mixture into the slow cooker. Cook on High for 1 hour, then reduce heat to Low and cook for 2 to 3 hours, or until a toothpick inserted into the center comes out clean and an instant-read thermometer inserted into the center reads 165 degrees F. Serve hot or at room temperature, with whipped cream if desired.

> While Panettone is the bread traditionally used in Italy for bread puddings, it's sometimes hard to find other than at Christmas time in many supermarkets. You can always substitute challah, brioche, or other rich egg breads.

Poached Figs with Toasted Pine Nuts and Mascarpone

This is a wonderful winter dessert: dried figs rehydrated in red wine flavored with cinnamon and citrus zest, and then topped with creamy cheese and crunchy pine nuts.

Makes 4 servings.

1 8-oz package dried Calimyrna figs

2 cups dry red wine

⅔ cup firmly packed light brown sugar

Two 3-inch cinnamon sticks

Two 3-inch strips lemon zest

Two 3-inch strips orange zest

½ cup pine nuts

½ pound mascarpone

1. Stem figs, and cut in half lengthwise. Set aside.

2. Combine wine and brown sugar in the slow cooker. Add figs, cinnamon sticks, lemon zest, and orange zest to the slow cooker, and stir well. Cook on Low for 4 to 6 hours, or on High for 2 to 3 hours, or until figs are very soft.

3. Remove and discard cinnamon sticks, lemon zest, and orange zest. Transfer figs to a bowl with a slotted spoon. Pour poaching liquid into a saucepan, and bring to a boil over medium-high heat. Cook for 10 minutes, stirring occasionally, or until liquid is reduced by half. Pour liquid over figs, and chill well.

4. While figs cook, place pine nuts in a dry skillet and cook over medium heat, stirring frequently, until brown. Set aside. To serve, spoon mascarpone over figs, and drizzle with poaching liquid. Sprinkle with pine nuts.

It's now much easier to find luscious and creamy mascarpone in supermarkets. But if you can't find it, its taste and texture can be replicated by mixing together an 8-ounce package cream cheese, ¼ pound unsalted butter, and 2 tablespoons sour cream or crème fraiche.

Amazing Almond Pudding Cake

The secret to this decadent delight? Amaretto. The Italian liqueur's toasted almond flavor infuses the pudding. Serve it warm topped with whipped cream or ice cream.

Makes 4 to 6 servings.

1 cup sugar

1 cup flour

¾ crushed amaretti cookies

2 teaspoons baking powder

⅓ cup whole milk

3 tablespoons unsalted butter, melted

2 tablespoons Amaretto

½ teaspoon almond extract

¾ cup firmly packed dark brown sugar

1¾ cup boiling water

Non-stick cooking spray

Whipped cream

1. Spray the inside of the slow cooker with non-stick cooking spray. Combine sugar, flour, crushed cookies, and baking powder in a mixing bowl. Stir in milk, melted butter, Amaretto, and almond extract. Stir until stiff batter forms. Spread batter in the slow cooker.

2. Sprinkle brown sugar over the batter, then pour the boiling water over it. Cover and cook on High for 2 to 2½ hours, or until a toothpick inserted into the top layer comes out clean. Allow pudding to sit for 15 minutes with slow cooker turned off before serving. Top with fresh whipped cream.

Amaretti are Italian almond-based macaroon cookies with a thin, crispy crust. They are typically served with coffee or a small glass of liqueur.

Chocolate Mousse

For a really elegant and decadent dessert, top light and fluffy chocolate mousse with fresh raspberries and whipped cream flavored with raspberry liqueur.

Makes 6 to 8 servings.

5 egg yolks

2 cups milk

½ cup sugar

1 teaspoon vanilla extract

¼ cup unsweetened cocoa powder

1. Put an oven-safe casserole dish into the slow cooker. Add water around the dish so that it reaches about halfway up the side of the dish.

2. In a large bowl, beat the egg yolks using a whisk until thoroughly combined and a lighter, lemony color. Add the milk, sugar, vanilla, and cocoa powder until well combined. Pour the mixture into the dish inside the slow cooker.

3. Cover and cook on Low for 5 to 6 hours or on High for 2 to 4 hours. The mousse should be thick but not too firm. Turn the cooker off and let the dish cool slightly in the water. Then remove it and refrigerate for an hour or longer before serving.

Flan

No cook is without plenty of eggs during the holidays. This classic custard recipe is another great way to use them to the delight of all who partake.

Makes 4 servings.

½ cup sugar
3 eggs
1/8 teaspoon salt
1½ cups whole milk
¾ teaspoon vanilla extract
Non-stick cooking spray

1. Spray the insides of four 6-oz ceramic ramekins with non-stick cooking spray and place them in the slow cooker. Add water slowly and carefully to go around the ramekins so that it comes about half way up the cups.

2. In a small skillet over medium heat, cook ¼ cup of the sugar until it melts into a light brown syrup, stirring constantly. Pour the syrup into the ramekins.

3. In a large bowl, combine eggs, salt, and another ¼ cup sugar. Beat with an electric mixer on low until the mixture is pale lemon-colored. With mixer still on low, gradually beat in milk and vanilla extract. When combined, distribute the mixture among the ramekins.

4. Cover and cook on Low for about 8 hours or on High for about 4 hours. Custards should be set but not overcooked. Remove and allow to cool. When serving, slide a knife around the rim to loosen the custard, and invert onto a plate so that the sugar syrup runs down the sides.

Variation:
For an added flavor boost, add 1 teaspoon lemon zest. Stir it in with the milk and vanilla toward the end of the instructions.

Festive Fruitcake

The slow cooker is an ideal vehicle for making this moist, fruit-dense dessert. There are many variations to fruit cake recipes, so if you don't like one of the ingredients, keep it out or substitute it with something you like.

Makes 8 to 10 servings.

1½ cup golden raisins
1 cup candied red and green cherries
¾ cup dates, pitted and chopped
¾ cup candied pineapple, diced
½ cup unsweetened coconut
3 cups flour
1 teaspoon baking powder
½ teaspoon salt
1 cup (8 tablespoon) butter, softened
1¼ cup sugar
1 teaspoon lemon zest
2 teaspoon lemon juice
4 eggs

1. Line the slow cooker with tin foil so the edges come up and over the sides. This will help you remove the cake when it's done.

2. Spray the foil lightly with non-stick cooking spray.

3. In a large bowl, combine the raisins, cherries, dates, pineapple, coconut, flour, baking powder, and salt. Set aside.

4. In another large bowl, cream the butter and sugar either by hand or with an electric mixer until combined and soft. Add the lemon zest and juice. Add the eggs one at a time, stirring until well combined before adding the next one.

5. Pour the dry ingredients into the bowl with the butter, and stir to mix everything without overdoing it.

6. Use a spatula to transfer the cake to the slow cooker. Cover and cook on Low for 4 to 6 hours. During the last 30 minutes, prop the lid open with the handle of a spoon or fork to allow some steam to escape. Use the foil edges to carefully lift the cake out of the slow cooker and transfer to a platter.

Index

About Cider Mill Press
Book Publishers

Good ideas ripen with time. From seed to harvest, Cider Mill Press brings fine reading, information, and entertainment together between the covers of its creatively crafted books. Our Cider Mill bears fruit twice a year, publishing a new crop of titles each spring and fall.

Visit us on the Web at
www.cidermillpress.com
or write to us at
12 Port Farm Road
Kennebunkport, Maine 04046